Their Blood
RUNS THRU US

STORIES OF LOVE, LOSS, AND LEGACY

Visionary

A M HOLLIDAY

Published by Victorious You Press™

Charlotte NC, USA

Copyright © 2023 **A M Holliday** All rights reserved.

No part of this book may be reproduced, distributed or transmitted in any form by any means, graphic, electronic, or mechanical, including photocopy, recording, taping, or by any information storage or retrieval system, without permission in writing from the author except in the case of reprints in the context of reviews, quotes, or references.

While the author has made every effort to ensure that the ideas, statistics, and information presented in this Book are accurate to the best of his/her abilities, any implications direct, derived, or perceived, should only be used at the reader's discretion. The author cannot be held responsible for any personal or commercial damage arising from communication, application, or misinterpretation of the information presented herein.

Unless otherwise indicated, scripture quotations are from the Holy Bible, King James Version. All rights reserved.

TITLE: THEIR BLOOD RUNS THRU US

First Printed: 2023

Cover Designer: Nadia Monsano

Editor: Charmaine LaFonde

ISBN: 978-1-952756-95-5

ISBN: (eBook) 978-1-952756-96-2

Library of Congress Control Number: 2023900371

Printed in the United States of America

For details email joan@victoriousyoupress.com
or visit us at www.victoriousyoupress.com

DEDICATION

This book is dedicated to every woman who has ever endured the pain of a loss but has continued to survive and thrive.

TABLE OF CONTENTS

Introduction 1

The Letter - Ebony Short 5

I Do This For Others, So That Others Will Do For You - Felicia Shingler . 17

You Carried Me, I Carried Them, - Nikeshia Pinnock Holt 29

Eight Months - Cheryl Livingston 37

Grief Beyond The Grave - Marsha Witherspoon 43

My Mom, My Friend, My Child - Wilma A. Pinnock 51

Empathy, Service And Love - AM Holliday 63

Motha - Katherine McCrary 78

Time - Angela Rouson 83

Call To Action 89

Resources 90

About The Authors 91

INTRODUCTION

When I Think of Death – By Maya Angelou

"When I think of death, and of late the idea has come with alarming frequency, I seem at peace with the idea that a day will dawn when I will no longer be among those living in this valley of strange humors. I can accept the idea of my own demise, but I am unable to accept the death of anyone else. I find it impossible to let a friend or relative go into that country of no return. Disbelief becomes my close companion, and anger follows in its wake. I answer the heroic question, "Death, where is thy sting?" with 'it is here in my heart and mind and memories.'"

Excerpt from WOULDN'T TAKE NOTHING FOR MY JOURNEY NOW by Maya Angelou, copyright @ 1993 by Maya Angelou. Used by permission of Random House, an imprint and division of Penguin Random House LLC. All rights reserved.

Who wants to talk about death, especially when it involves the death of a close loved one? Nobody, that's who! Nobody wants to talk about death or even deal with it until it is thrust upon them. It's like walking by the cosmetics counter in a department store and suddenly becoming overwhelmed by a strong, intrusive fragrance which was just sprayed. We become overwhelmed while in the midst of it. While making funeral arrangements, or caring for the family members left behind, when is there time to process the loss? We hear the comments of those who come to comfort us, but really don't know what to say.

"They're in a better place now."

"You must move on."

"Get over it."

But when all is said and done, we also experience the deafening silence which comes after everyone is gone. When there are no more phone calls, and no more messages asking about our well-being, where does it leave us? Do we feel alone, overwhelmed, depressed, or even angry? It's not unusual to feel lost and unsure about what to do next, but it is my hope that this book will help to change that.

I lost my mother over ten years ago. Since that time, I have become keenly aware of the unspoken struggles we face when someone close to us dies. Everyone grieves differently, so you really don't know how long the grieving process will take until you experience it for yourself. It's been my experience that most people shy away from the topic and don't know how to interact with those who are going through the grieving process. It's like they think death might rub off on them if they say the word or show post-funeral compassion. I was inspired to create this anthology to not only share stories about grief, but to give those who have experienced a significant loss an opportunity to share their memories and the legacy left behind by their loved one. Each of these stories reveal a common thread we share when struggling with grief and loss, and captured in each story is a path which points in the direction to grief recovery.

"When we lose someone, we love, we must learn not to live without them, but to live with the love they left behind."

-Unknown

> "...Daughter, your faith has healed you. Go in peace and be freed from your suffering."
> -Mark 5:34 (NIV)

THE LETTER
Ebony Short

I find it extremely difficult to properly address this letter to you as I refer to you as "your father" when speaking with my siblings about you. It's always "your husband," when speaking to my mother about you. I rarely refer to you as "Dad" or "Father" because you never displayed any of the characteristics associated with the title, so rather than address you at all, I will simply begin writing.

There were not too many moments in my life when I can recall you being sober. Those moments were very few and far between. When mom changed the locks to our apartment door to prevent you from coming and going as you pleased, I was in the second grade. Your presence always ushered in heartache, suffering, and the smell of addiction, so despite the somberness of the day and the sadness I saw in my mother's eyes, when that old lock was discarded, I sensed a bit of relief from everyone.

The dysfunctional and disruptive behavior you displayed throughout our lives as a result of your alcohol addiction created many painful memories. A few months before our mother evicted you, she had undergone major surgery and not once did you visit us. You didn't visit her while she was hospitalized, and during her long recovery, you didn't bother to check on her or our well-being. Thankfully friends blessed our family during that traumatic period ensuring that we had food, clothes, and attended school as our mother recovered.

Michelle, Eddie, and Darryl were eleven, ten and seven years older than me respectively, so they had already experienced the painful consequences of your addiction prior to my birth. It wasn't until I was around eleven years old that I began to fully see you as the non-functioning alcoholic that you were. It wasn't until then that I began to feel the same pain that they and our mother had already experienced. You were not just any non-functioning alcoholic, you were an addict who shared in my being, incapable of fulfilling the role of the father that I always dreamed of having.

Not only did you have to live with that horrific disease but everyone who knew you, especially your immediate family, had to live with the painful consequences of your addiction. Our mother struggled to care for us as we lived in poverty and felt totally abandoned by you even when you lived with us. I despised hearing you lie to others about how you provided for us when you actually left us to be with other women, or you stayed out drinking all night only to return acting as if you never left. The most painful consequence as a result of your absence in our lives was that you never showed up for our birthdays, holidays, school activities, or even when we were sick. None of us wanted to become an alcoholic like you, and we cringed at even the thought of taking even a sip of alcohol. I am passionate about educating your grandchildren about the genetic traits of alcoholism, and I am constantly in prayer that none of them follow your path.

Those who have never lived with an addict, have no idea how great the pain is for those of us who have. As a child, I struggled with the notion that you choose alcohol over our family and allowed your addiction to cause significant pain in our lives. The pain inflicted by your choice continues somewhat to this day. When I recall how you yelled loudly with slurred speech and stumbled with every step through the house nude, even in the presence of company, I cringe. I can't help but think about what a negative impact your actions had on all of us when you were intoxicated-- totally obliterated, and oblivious to your surroundings. A taker is how I would describe you. You left very few positive deposits in our lives, and I never saw you purchase food, clothes, or medicine for us. You didn't help pay bills and you didn't support or encourage us.

"Does your mother have a boyfriend?" was the only thing you were concerned about after you two were separated. After the way you treated her, she deserved someone in life to encourage her and make her smile. I wished she did have someone to pray with her and for her, but rather than seek the companionship of another man, she chose to put all her energy into raising us to become productive. Many of our neighbors were dependent on government assistance and ridiculed our mother for leaving home early in the morning to go to work. They also mocked her as she rushed home from work every evening to make sure we had a home cooked meal. Without any support from you, our mother found the strength that only God could give to also review our homework for accuracy and completeness, and make sure we were prepared for the next day.

Single parenting is filled with many challenges, but our mother showed us that all things are possible with determination and God's grace and mercy. My mother recovered without your help or the help of any other man and proved herself to be an amazing provider. You didn't think she would be able to do it without a man's help, but when you counted her down and out, she did not allow your negativity to drive her into despair. The American dream of home ownership became her reality, in spite of the fact that you obviously didn't know her strength or believe in her. Thank God when you counted her down and out it became the fuel she used which propelled us out of poverty and into a safer neighborhood.

I was in the eleventh grade when you survived that brutal attack which left you confined to a wheelchair. You were intoxicated in the wrong place, at the wrong time, and suffered head trauma as a result of that beating. I became hopeful for a new beginning while you were recovering from that attack. I was anticipating the time when we would bond as father and daughter, and when you finally secured that apartment that accommodated the disabled, I was ecstatic for you. Every Saturday, I did not mind making that two-hour journey, each way, to visit you because that was our time to finally bond. Every week when I visited you and pushed your wheelchair a few blocks down the street to purchase groceries, it dawned on me one day that you purchased very little food, but purchasing beer was your number one priority. Your priority was that same beer that caused you to be in the wrong place at the wrong time which resulted in you being permanently confined to a wheelchair.

In that moment, it hit me. You were choosing that same beer, along with other spirits, that caused you to neglect your wife and children, and as I pushed you back home to your apartment, watching how you began consuming the same beer that meant more to you than your family, I felt hope slip away. I became extremely disheartened and disappointed at the thought that you would probably never become the father I longed for. My heart began to sink when I thought about how I would never have that father to walk me down the aisle someday; and I would never have the father I deserved. Sadly, I followed the same path as my siblings before me had done, and I chose to alienate you. I did it for the sake of my broken heart.

Shortly after I joined rank with my siblings in keeping my distance from you to allow time for my heart to heal from the disappointment, several family members began calling and insisting that we visit you. Each time they called, I explained how painful those visits with you were for me. They were persistent in their efforts to get us to visit you, but I wondered if they were as persistent when it came to encouraging you to go home and check on us—your children—your wife—your family, during those times when you were absent from our lives for days, weeks and months at a time. Did they insist that you seek help for your addiction? Yes, I had my reasons for not wanting to see you and I didn't want to feel pressured into doing something I did not have the heart to do, so I began avoiding them and their phone calls. I cringed at their conversations about how smart you were when you were younger and how you were admired by so many. They painted such a rosy picture of who you were, but they failed to mention how you were a mentally abusive alcoholic who was never there for your wife and children.

When you were diagnosed with throat cancer, that's when Big Momma contacted me and pleaded with me to visit you. Her main concern was that after your laryngectomy I would never be able to hear your voice again. That's what it meant to Big Momma. What it meant to me was I would no longer have to hear lies coming from your mouth. You were losing your voice, but I would be losing the painful conversations we always had. At the time, I didn't acknowledge how serious your diagnosis was or the possibility that you could possibly die from it, and although it was selfish on my part, I don't even recall praying for you.

A few years later, when you were once again hospitalized, it was Big Momma who reached out to me to visit you. When I learned you were hospitalized at the same hospital where I worked, I was concerned. My main concern, when I came to visit you, was leaving before I encountered anyone who might question our relationship. I was ashamed to be your daughter, and I definitely didn't want my coworkers to notice that we shared the same last name. Although you were near death as a result of cancer, I knew that the type of cancer that had consumed your body was linked to chronic alcohol consumption and cigarette smoking. Those were the things that meant more to you than your family, and when I received the news of your death, I had no feelings whatsoever. I felt no pain, no sorrow, nothing good, nothing bad—I felt nothing.

Your siblings contacted us shortly after your death to ask us to share the costs of your funeral expenses. I refused. I didn't feel you deserved a funeral. "Just bury him"! is exactly what I felt, and even though I was reluctant to do so, I eventually decided to attend your funeral.

On the day of your funeral, I passed the church while in route to Big Momma's house and noticed the large number of cars which had arrived early for your service. When I arrived at Big Momma's house, I met Monique, the daughter you created with another woman four years prior to my birth. I was excited to meet her because I always knew she existed. My mother never spoke of her, but I often gazed at the picture of her as a young child that sat on Eddie's and Darryl's chest of drawers. As excited as I was to meet her for the first time, her response to me was not a very warm one.

I asked her where she lived. "In the city," was her cold response. My spirit was immediately broken. I didn't understand her cold demeanor and why she was upset with me, so, for the rest of the day, I ignored her. We sat next to each other in the family car and at the service, but I acted as if she were not even there.

Upon arriving at the church, I could not understand why such a huge assembly of people were gathered there to honor your life. How could there be such an outpouring of love and support for the father who was never there for us? The more I tried to understand, the more I felt my spirit being crushed. I walked into the church and saw the faces of so many family members and others unknown to me who had gathered in mourning and my eyes quickly locked on the beautiful rich solid wood mahogany casket that laid ahead of me. I looked beyond the sight of your lifeless body lying there and was flabbergasted that anyone would choose to place your body in such a breathtaking vessel which seemed only fit for royalty. I sat between Darryl and Monique, and I tried my best not to touch her. I ignored her tears but wondered what kind of relationship the two of you shared that would cause her to be so sad that you were gone.

At your burial site, when I heard Michelle crying out over the voice of the pastor, she wasn't sobbing loudly because she was sad, she was upset that people kept calling you a good man. She listened attentively to what others were saying about you and rather than mourn the fact that you were gone, she was feeling the agony that you had caused her entire life. Unlike Michelle, I didn't shed a tear that day, but I totally understood her pain.

When we gathered at the family home after the funeral, I gazed into the face of every woman I didn't recognize. I was wondering which one was Monique's mother.

"How's your mother doing?" I heard several family members ask Monique. So, the family I had known all of my life was smiling and asking the sister I just met, about the woman that you cheated on my mother with? It seemed apparent to me that my family shared an intimate relationship with Monique and her mother and somehow felt comfortable acknowledging their existence in my presence. I spun into a whirlwind of thoughts about what I never knew about Monique. I wondered did she spend time with *my* grandparents, aunts, uncles, and cousins? Did she spend several weeks at the farm each summer as I did? Were you a better father to her than you were to me and my other siblings? Did she grow up with a silver spoon in her mouth? Was she also baptized at the family church? I had so many questions then, and years later, those same questions lingered in my mind.

I ran into Monique again five years later at a family reunion, and we had a chance to speak privately about our interaction at your funeral. She shared she wasn't mad at me, but at the time, she was just sad to learn that you had never married her mother, among other things. We both shared a lot of information with each other that day which had been swept under the rug for decades. She learned that although you and my mother were separated for many years, you were still legally married. She had the impression that Michelle, Eddie, Darryl, and I grew up with silver spoons in our mouths, and I laughed at how far from the truth that notion was.

Monique and I created a bond, over time, and a few years before Michelle's death, the three of us met for lunch and a beautiful sisterly bond formed. Michelle and Eddie were my biggest supporters and cheerleaders and when they passed, I honestly didn't know how I would survive without them. Monique was there for me and has truly become the co-captain on my cheerleading team. She has been a listening ear and is always offering big sister advice. I was twenty-two years old when I met her and even though we didn't develop a sisterly relationship until nearly ten years later, it feels like we have been in each other's lives since birth. For that, I will be forever grateful.

When I first accepted a position working in a Hepatitis C clinic, I had no idea that a significant amount of my patients would be alcoholics. Many of them visited the clinic on a weekly basis and then transitioned to monthly visits. Most of my patients were monitored while undergoing treatment for up to eighteen months. My patients opened up to me, many of them sharing their life experiences. I heard about their new jobs, promotions, significant others, children, grandchildren, vacations, family celebrations, hardships, and struggles. I also heard numerous stories of how many of them were able to claim victory over addiction while others shared their daily struggles with it. Many revealed that they really desired to stop using drugs and/or drinking alcohol but couldn't due to very strong urges, weakness and the euphoric feeling that they experienced while being high.

A lot of my patients, talked to me about the shame and guilt they carried as a result of not being the spouses, parents, and employees they knew they should have been, and even though I was hearing their stories day after day, I never thought of you or wondered if you shared those same sentiments. Prior to the time when I accepted that job assignment, I really couldn't understand why you couldn't just put the bottle down and be the father we so desperately needed. I was attending a spiritual retreat with some other women when God revealed to me why he had placed me in that clinic. I was there so that I could learn that alcoholism is a disease, and you did love me--in spite of your actions.

That revelation positioned me to surrender and release a significant amount of pain and hurt to God. I instantly felt tons of weight lifted from my heart. I realized I never hated you, but I did yearn for your love, attention, support and presence, which you were never able to give because of your disease. As I matured and studied God's words, I learned that difficult times will come, but during those times we must seek relief, comfort, refuge, and resolutions from God through prayer. We must trust and believe that our heavenly father would never leave us or forsake us no matter how painful life may be. God is in the midst of every circumstance and there is purpose in every situation we face.

Writing this letter to you has truly been very therapeutic. I have been able to let go of even more pain, and I am thankful to God for giving me more days to learn how to release the pain that I allowed to make me bitter. I am better equipped and able to show love to others, to forgive, and to simply be a better person in HIS eyes.

In your absence, I learned to trust God in all situations and to talk with, listen to and to obey Him. When I am lonely, he comforts me. When I cry, he dries my tears. When I feel pain (physical and psychological), he comforts me. When I am hungry, he feeds me. He has fulfilled every need I have ever had. There is no greater love that a child can have than that of our heavenly Father and I am thankful that He never fails. There is truly comfort in knowing God, watching him deliver over and over and seeing every promise in the Holy Bible fulfilled.

With God's grace and mercy, we are able to grow through everything we go through, and today, I am truly grateful for my growth. It has helped me to be the servant I was called to be. I can now look past the shortcomings of others, acknowledge my own, and pray for us all through this journey. I have learned to pray instead of having pity parties and I have learned to welcome God's presence in all that I do. Blocking out negative thoughts and deeds are a part of my walk, and although I may never fully understand this walk, I know we are all born with purpose, even addicts. Sometimes goodness has to be prayed out instead of blocked in and I failed to help pray it out of you. As a child, I didn't understand the power of prayer, but I have learned that it works. I don't know if others prayed for you or if you even prayed for yourself, but I do pray at this time that your soul be at peace. I now know that healing doesn't always take place on this earth but for some, healing does not come until death. May you rest in peace!

Until we meet again,

Ebony

"Strength and honour are her clothing; and she shall rejoice in time to come. She openeth her mouth with wisdom; and in her tongue is the law of kindness. She looketh well to the ways of her household, and eateth not the bread of idleness. Her children arise up, and call her blessed."

-Proverbs 31: 25-28 (KJV)

I DO THIS FOR OTHERS, SO THAT OTHERS WILL DO FOR YOU
Felicia Shingler

My mother could find the good in any situation, and everyone who knew her attests to her kindness. I was twenty-nine years old when she died at the age of 62. I was reminiscing about my mother over dinner with a friend who knew her.

"I loved your mother because when you came into her house everyone was her child. We were all her children," my high school friend shared with me.

"Ohhh!!! She absolutely loved you and your brother!" I exclaimed; and from across the dinner table, just as warm and kind as my mother's hugs were, my high school friend concurred, "We could feel it!"

My house was a place where my friends from elementary school, middle school, high school, and even a few of my college friends felt welcome. Mom would most likely be sitting at the dining room table reading the paper when my friends came by. Either that, or she was on the living room couch with her feet propped up, doing what she loved, reading. In our living room stood a bookshelf that was seven feet tall and three feet wide. I never noticed the diverse book titles until one of my college buddies, who had just received his civil engineering degree, commented on the interesting and impressive display of books. The bookshelf contained Ralph Ellison's, *The Invisible Man*; John Hope Franklin's, *From Slavery to Freedom*; Booker T. Washington's, *The Story of the Negro* and *Up From Slavery*; various Harlequin romance novels; Maya Angelo's, *And Still I Rise*; two half sets of encyclopedias: (the blue one was Britannica and the orange one was *Funk and Wagnall's*); the *Home Remedies Almanac*; at least two dictionaries; a couple of books by Dr. Spock, and a host of other books. My mom's subscriptions to *Psychology Today* and *Forbes* magazine, both had a place on the crowded bookshelf.

My mother packed me and my girlfriends into her lime green Ford Pinto and drove us all over the city. We went shopping, to lunches and dinners, and even to Kings Dominion in that lime green Pinto. One year my best friend and I wanted to take a trip to Hawaii or California to celebrate our high school graduation. My mother encouraged us to work during the summer to earn money to pay for our trip, so we delivered phone books from the hatch of her car. It was hard work for two 17-year-old, 90 to 120-pound girls and an aging, somewhat round 5-foot-tall woman, but it taught us a few valuable lessons. First of all, hard work pays off, and often in ways we may not have expected. Another valuable lesson we learned as we worked towards our goal was that nothing in this life is free. You have to work for what you want. Now, I do not remember going on the trip, but I do remember having a super, fantastic, knock-down, drag-out party at the end of the phonebook tour which happened just before our senior school year began.

My mother was gracious enough to allow one of my girlfriends permission to drive her Pinto! At the time, I only had my learner's driving permit, so I couldn't drive without a licensed adult with me, but my girlfriend had her license to drive. My mother allowed my licensed friend and me to travel by ourselves and we went all over the District, Maryland, and Virginia (DMV) area. When the Congressional Black Caucus met in early fall at the Sheraton off of Connecticut Avenue in D.C., my girlfriends and I put on our pretty dresses, heels, and our mothers' mink stoles, got in the Pinto, drove from Southern Avenue and crashed the Congressman's wives' after parties. Little did we know we were being groomed to work on Capitol Hill, communicate with all echelons of society, minister to the lost, and sit on numerous boards.

On other occasions, we put on our designer party clothes and headed to the club. I remember having a lavender, silk dress from Saks Fifth Avenue that one of my older cousins got for me. I wore that dress with pearls, stockings, and 3-inch pumps with a clutch bag to match, and once we were all dressed to the nines, we piled into that Pinto and headed to the Black Crystal Night Club. Unbeknownst to us, my mother's co-worker was a bouncer at the club. We were sixteen years old and had no idea that Mom ensured our safety in that adult atmosphere with her co-worker acting as our bodyguard.

When we got back from our outing at the club, before I had a chance to tell my story, my girlfriends told my mother all about our night. I mean, I remember being upstairs in the bathroom of our little 2-story, basement included townhouse listening to them recant our evening and me yelling down to them.

"Can I tell *my* mother *my* story, please?"

They laughed and continued telling her about the evening. When I finally joined them, my mother graciously listened to me re-tell the story from the beginning to the end from my perspective.

I had attended college, was married, had my first child, and had brought a house two-doors down from my mother's house. One young woman, who was a single-parent, also lived in our neighborhood. She worked at a job that required her to be at work at 7:00 in the morning. My mother was retired and had no reason to get up early unless she wanted to, but she got up early in the morning to drive our neighbor to her job. When our neighbor was between paydays, my mom loaned her money and sometimes even gave her small gifts, just to encourage her. I was very aware of my mom's kindness, and one day I asked her about it.

"Mom, why are you so kind to our neighbor? You seem to go out of your way for her." She shrugged and responded with the utmost tenderness.

"I do this for her so that others might do it for you."

I often heard her say that when she was doing for others. My mother was kind, generous, and gracious to everyone who crossed her path. For most people, it is easier to do for folks when it is convenient, however, my mom went out of her way to help those in need.

My first job was a candy striper at Cafritz Hospital. My next job, which I loved, was a retail position at Phillipsborn in Eastover Shopping Center and paid a whopping $3.10 per hour. Back then, Phillipsborn was a high-end woman's fashion store which catered to the upper middle-class community. Most of the shoppers who came into my store were white women. I was one of two blacks that worked in the store and, at seventeen years old, I decided I wanted to be in fashion retail.

"No! You will not pursue a job that calls you to stand on your feet all day and barely make enough money to support you in life!" my mother told me.

"You are either going to college or you are going to work in the federal government," she said.

I did both. During that summer, I worked for the federal government as an aide at the National Institutes of Health (NIH). Before the age of laptops, fax machines, e-mail, and cell phones, any messages or packages were delivered in person. My immediate supervisor, responsible for the oversight of the blue-collar and administrative employees, often sent me across the beautiful NIH campus to deliver paperwork to the offices she supported. I was happy with my assignments and performed each of them with diligence and excellence, then eagerly awaited the next one.

One day, in order to allow herself more time to prepare my next assignment, my supervisor suggested that I visit with a cousin of mine, who worked in another building on the campus. In addition, she was aware that my aunt also worked on the campus.

My aunt worked in the building which housed the NIH director and other prestigious employees. She was the first Black to work in that building in a position other than in the mailroom or a member of the housekeeping staff. She worked in the Committee Management Office, so I visited her and her co-workers for a few minutes before making my way back to my office for my next assignment.

I got accepted into Drexel University and Virginia Tech, but I chose to attend Drexel because their curriculum allowed me to pursue my fashion retail and business acumen. Drexel's cooperative agreement program mandated students attend school for six months and then work, preferably in their field of study, for the remaining six months of the year. After my first year at Drexel, where freshmen had to complete at least three terms before going on co-op assignments, I returned to my federal government job at the NIH in the same administrative office where I worked previously as a summer aide. I was able to begin my co-op assignment after my supervisor at the NIH granted me an extension from the summer internship of an additional three months.

My experience in working at the NIH brings to mind an example of my mother's mantra of "I do this for them so that others would do it for my child." The NIH had a training program which allowed employees to transition from a lower-level pay grade into the higher paying professional series. It was a very competitive program and every year, from a pool of 300 to 500 applications, only five jobs were announced, although not always filled. I applied for an administrative assistant position and a writer/editor position. I landed the writer/editor position.

The outgoing manager, who loved the status and connections associated with being the NIH Activity Codes Manager, was assigned to train me thoroughly. He very reluctantly obliged.

In my new position as the NIH Activity Codes Manager, I was responsible for creating activity codes and committee management codes. I was new and had no idea how to create the committee management codes, so with a wave of his hand, my trainer dismissively directed me to call someone for the codes. I was unsure of how to get the codes, so I called the committee management office and tried to explain what I needed from them. The voice on the other end of the phone was harsh and raspy and fired several questions at me which I hesitantly responded.

I explained that I was new to the job and had only been to Building One when I worked as a summer aide to visit my aunt who was now retired.

"Your aunt!? What was her name?" she asked, curiously surprised. When I told her who my aunt was, her whole demeanor changed! I could hear her excitedly say to the other employees in the office, "It's Felicia! Albertha's niece. Hurry, let's get her what she needs!"

My first supervisor encouraged me to visit my aunt, which was a valuable lesson in networking. Ten years later the networking paid off. Those same women in my aunt's office helped me navigate my first professional assignment and willingly showed me all I needed to know about my job as it related to their office. That was God's favor and I believe they did for me because my mother did for others.

A few years later, my mother died, which caused me to become very angry. I was angry at my mother for leaving me suddenly. I was lost. I was in shock. I was in disbelief. I could not believe she left me. Why would she leave me? I could not understand it.

We were preparing to celebrate the birthday of my oldest son. He was going to be seven years old, and we were organizing an outdoor pirate-themed sleepover to be held at my mother's house on the following day. I called her at 5:30 that morning and when she didn't answer the phone, I thought, "Hmmm, I guess she is not up yet or in the bathroom." I got my kids up, fed and dressed them, and walked my oldest son to the school bus stop which was right in front of my mom's house. I knocked on her door and the dog barked and jumped up at the doorknob. Even though I had a key, the night latch was engaged. My mom did not answer the door. I went home and called her again...still no answer.

My husband had already left for work, so I took my younger son to the babysitter who was just ten minutes away from our house. I shared my concern with the babysitter and also let her know what my next move was going to be.

"If she doesn't respond when I go back to her house, I'm going to break the door down." I told her.

Back at my mom's house, the dog was still at the front door. I could see him at the window and through the crack when I unlocked the door with my key. I put my shoulder to the wooden door and burst the night lock off and went into my mother's house. I called out. There was no answer. I went upstairs and there she was. Asleep? No, she was dead. She had died in her sleep. It was so natural, yet unreal. I had just been with her the day before. I said good night over the hedge and we talked for ten more minutes after saying goodnight. My last words to her were, "Good night, Mom. See you in the morning."

Three years earlier, my father died, so when my mother died, it was like someone pulled a rug out from under me. While I was proceeding through the probate process, the estate sale, Goodwill donations, and managing my mother's accounts, I was slowly losing control. My mother had always been my support system; she had always been my lifeline. When my mother died my life began to swing wildly out of control. I was disoriented, confused, and spiraled into an abyss of loneliness and grief. When my parents were alive, I was fearless because I knew they always had my back, but suddenly I found myself emotionally wrecked, feeling unloved, exposed, unprotected, and without any guidance.

One day after I had just picked up my youngest son from daycare, I was almost home when police cars, ambulances, and fire trucks whizzed by me with sirens blaring. I pulled my car over to the right side of the street to allow the emergency vehicles to pass and as I did that, I felt my neck and shoulders tense up. The tense sensation moved down my back and met with the sinking feeling I had in the pit of my stomach. Something was wrong. Something had happened to something, or someone attached to me. As I approached the intersection of Southern Avenue and Owens Road, I felt sick. I stopped the car, grabbed my son out of his car seat and ran across the street, which was now blocked by the emergency vehicles that had just sped by me. I saw someone laid out on a stretcher and before I could identify who it was, I already knew it was my nine-year-old.

"Oh, God!" I screamed.

"What is happening? What's going on?"

I was still carrying my three-year old in my arms and as I hysterically screamed, he began to cry and scream along with me.

I found out that my oldest son had been crossing Southern Avenue to play with his friends when he was hit by a car. He was transported by helicopter to Children's Hospital and by the grace of God, there were no head injuries and no broken bones. The muscle that attached his tongue to his mouth was torn, and other than bruises to his face, he survived.

That accident was my wake-up call, and it brought me back to reality and back to God. After my mother's death, I made a pit stop between her death and finding my way back to God. The pit stop created isolation, and what my pastor calls, 'only-Itis'. Only-Itis is when you feel like you are the only one who is or who has ever gone through what you are experiencing. Ahhh... the devil loves isolation. It is in that place of isolation where he does his best work. That is the place where he can kill, steal, and destroy. He wants you to think you are alone and no one understands how you feel. The more one stays in a place of isolation, the more he can torment and whisper in your ear.

"No one understands how you feel, or how much you miss your mother because she's *YOUR* mother, not theirs." Let's be honest; when it comes to grieving a loss, you have a right to feel exactly what and how you feel. Take as long as it takes to process the pain, loneliness, bewilderment, or fill in the blank with what you are feeling. It took me twenty years to accept my mother's passing. When my 57-pound, 2-and-a-half-foot-tall, 9-year-old got hit by a 3000-pound Toyota Corolla and miraculously sustained only minor injuries, I knew God was throwing me a lifeline and I knew I was not alone. I went back to my home church and never left God again.

I began to heal. Yes, I still missed my mother, but God's grace was so sincere, kind, gentle, and comforting that I was able to come back to myself. I sincerely believe that Jesus is seated on the right hand of God interceding for me. I once again had someone in my corner. I can climb up in his lap and curl up in that fetal position; just like I could come home and sit at the dining room table and talk to my mother. Jesus is always there to listen to my stories even though he already knows what I'm going to say.

When I returned to God and started fellowshipping again with other like-minded believers, I began to feel the love, security, and protection I thought I had lost in the passing of my mother. I had the Holy Spirit to lead me, which meant I was available to love and care for others the way Jesus loved and cared for me. The Holy Spirit sustained me, or as the saints would say, "He kept me". The hole left in my heart by my mother's passing, was filled by the Holy Spirit and, by doing so, he made me whole again. Not only did I learn to praise, worship, and journal my prayers to God, but I also learned that life was not about me, but about serving others. When I stepped into that place of service to others, it took the spotlight off of me and my loss.

My mother has been gone longer than I had her with me. I miss her and remember her being the nicest person I've ever known, and I aspire to be as kind, generous, and gracious as she was. I have a long way to go to fill her shoes, but in the meantime, I do for others in hopes that others will do for my children and grandchildren. I do this for them that they might do for mine to continue my mother's legacy which somehow keeps her with me. Her blood, her kindness, her legacy runs through me. She is with me still.

"In life I loved you dearly, in death I love you still; In my heart you hold a place no one else could ever fill."
-Unknown

YOU CARRIED ME, I CARRIED THEM,
Nikeshia Pinnock Holt

In Loving Honor of Cristina Young

Motherhood is a beautiful blessing from God. Being able to conceive and carry a child in the womb is a priceless miracle. Women of girl children up the ante by not only carrying their daughters in their womb, but their grandchildren as well. Confused? This is my favorite fun fact. A female fetus develops a full reproductive system by or around twenty weeks gestation and is born with six to seven million egg cells in their ovaries. This means, every maternal grandmother has carried their grandchild in their womb.

I often wondered if that was the reason why I was so close to my grandmother. In every significant (and not so significant) moment of my life, my grandmother was there. First day of school, there. First ballet recital, there. First period, there. Graduation, there, times three! Marriage, there. Yet, as time progressed, so did she. My grandmother progressed, and so did the sickness, confusion, aggression, and hopelessness. The strongest person I knew was fighting a losing battle, and because of that, I lost her twice. Right before my eyes, dementia snatched the mind, body, and soul from my grandmother. She was my heart and my favorite shoulder to cry on, and my loving memories of her become distorted and overshadowed by the beast that invaded her psyche. I saw it in her void eyes, her unfamiliar touch, and her suspicious tone. My grandmother was no longer able to control her shifts in mood and behavior, and it was a painful experience when she could no longer remember or recognize me. I couldn't accept that our bond was breaking. How could she not remember how it felt to carry me in her womb? How could she do this to me while my own womb was struggling, breaking, and letting go? How was I to mourn her and them at the same time?

It wasn't fair to blame her. I'd witnessed her prayers to God to "not end up like those people." It hurt me to see my grandmother, my queen, in so much pain and misery, so I had to remind myself of the bountiful wisdom she'd instilled in me throughout my life. She was my caretaker, so I became hers. No amount of errand running, senior center drop-offs and pick-ups, or bath and bedtime assistance would ever amount to what she provided me. She was the spiritual guide who taught me about faith, intuition, and prayer; so, when she was in pain, I prayed for her. I spoke peace over her, and life into her. I prayed for God's favor or a miracle. At some point, I stopped being selfish and began to pray for her happiness. I prayed for her pain to go away and that she be released from the restraints of the beast that terrorized her daily. While I was mourning the loss of the woman I once knew, who two generations ago carried me as an egg then later raised me, I had to once again let go. The last time I saw her "alive" I read her favorite scripture in her ear and said goodbye for what I knew would be the last time. When I left her presence, my spirit was as light as hers was because we both knew her season of suffering would soon be over.

STAGES OF GRIEF

In 1969, Psychologist Elizabeth Kubler-Ross introduced the 5-step model of death and dying which examined the psychological response for patients facing an impending death. As years progressed, this concept broadened and is now also applied to grief. Her theory details five stages: (1) Denial, (2) Anger, (3) Bargaining, (4) Depression, and (5) Acceptance. An individual may experience these stages in any order.

Denial is one of the most commonly used defense mechanisms. Denial protects us from the truth when we do not want to face reality. Though it is common, it is not healthy to stay in denial. To the not so keen eye, my grandmother's denial appeared in the form of frustration. Tiny moments of memory lapses caused her to stomp a foot, suck her teeth, or rub her eyebrows.

"I don't know what's happening with my brain," she would say, and then proceed to try to explain the momentary lapses. She blamed her lapses on not drinking enough water, or sleepiness, or even blaming her prescription medication. I chalked it all up to old age and never gave it a second thought. It certainly didn't dawn on me that it could be anything more serious than that because, who doesn't forget things from time to time? Right?

Eventually, the tiny moments of forgetfulness morphed into larger and more frequent occurrences. Grandma started to repeat herself more often than usual and started to show signs of cognitive dysfunction. Feeling that control slipping away caused her temperament to often turn to displays of aggression and lots of curse words. Stages of anger appear once denial is reconciled. I began to grow impatient with her and didn't notice that she sometimes struggled because she was confusing the house phone with the TV remote. She began to be so obsessed over not being able to finish a crossword puzzle, and I could not understand why. After I gave birth to my daughter, I began to understand my grandmother's frustration. She could not fend for herself the way she used to, and I empathized with her feelings of not wanting to be a burden on anyone. The bargaining stage of grief is an attempt to regain a sense of control.

I believe my grandmother was aware of what was happening but didn't quite know how to articulate it. Whenever she watched a movie or show on TV which involved an elderly person suffering with dementia, she prayed that she never be met with a fate like that. As her episodes of confusion, delusion, and paranoia increased, she began to bargain with God to exchange peace for her moments of physical pain or mental anguish. In time, I recognized the amount of agony my grandmother was in and did what I considered to be the mature and selfless thing by asking God to give me some of her pain; I no longer wanted to watch her suffer.

In my defense, I didn't know that dying could hurt so bad. I guess there was still some denial within me because I didn't think God would make her suffer for so long before He called her Home. During my grandmother's final months, we were both depressed. I had yet again experienced a pregnancy loss, and she was yet again hospitalized. I guess we clung onto each other's vulnerability at the time.

I remember this one particular day that plays on a loop in my head. My grandmother and I were alone in her hospital room. After I had prayed over her and read her favorite scripture to her, she looked at me with the saddest eyes I had ever seen on her, and she told me she wished she could die. She was ready to see her mother, and I guess that was also her way of acceptance.

There is no timeframe for the five stages of grief, and it is totally acceptable to work through them at your own pace. The day will come when I will be able to accept that my grandmother is really gone, but for now, I'm happy knowing she is no longer suffering.

SO, YOU'VE LOST SOMEONE YOU LOVE. NOW WHAT?

I never thought I would appreciate a bouquet of flowers so much. As the family came together to prepare for my grandmother's homegoing service, we spent a lot of time reminiscing about her. Our time together was filled with so much love and laughter as we sat together and watched videos and looked at old pictures of a healthy and present version of our grandmother. The healthy version of my grandmother's face is the face I see in my dreams. Grief isn't fair, and despite the theories on grief, there's no fool-proof manual for it.

Although that week of preparation was more bearable than I anticipated, I was not at all prepared for the overwhelming amount of well-intended comments aimed to comfort me, but clearly missed the mark. Let me offer a bit of advice – when attempting to console someone who is grieving, please do not say "Everything happens for a reason." You can also keep the "God doesn't make mistakes" comments to yourself. I found that the kindest and most sincere comments came from those who personally understood what it meant to lose a loved one. Being open and vulnerable is a challenge, but those genuine moments and conversations left a lasting impression and encouraged me to seek help with processing such a dramatic loss. I leaned into the things my grandmother taught me, like how to talk to God and how to listen to my spirit. My spiritual awareness has blossomed as I began to carry out the legacy of the many lessons, she taught me.

GETTING HELP AND MOVING FORWARD

Now, I must learn one of the only lessons that my grandmother didn't teach me; how to navigate life without her presence. Communication has been a priority during this process. I've been able to help others help me by being specific about what I needed to advance my healing. I speak up when I am feeling down, and on tough days I give myself plenty of grace.

My grandmother raised me, and she will always have her own special space in my heart. Needless to say, it was a no-brainer that my daughter would be her namesake. As an added bonus, my daughter fully embodies my grandmother's personality, humor, and soul. Her legacy lives on through her granddaughter and great-granddaughter.

We love you.

"Therefore, you now have sorrow; but I will see you again and your heart will rejoice, and your joy no one will take from you."
-John 16:22 (NKJV)

EIGHT MONTHS
Cheryl Livingston

It was the evening of Super Bowl XXXVIII, February 1, 2004, and my family gathered at the bedside of my sister. She was in so much pain as she awaited the birth of her first-born child. We sat around with her, watched the game, witnessed Janet Jackson's wardrobe malfunction during the halftime show, and patiently waited for the baby to make its appearance. After a long evening at the hospital, the doctor finally released my sister to go home. There was going to be no baby born that night.

The very next day, Groundhog Day, we all headed back to the hospital to witness the birth of my nephew. I was in the delivery room when he was born and I thought I was going to pass out! My mom and I assisted in coaching my nephew out and I had the pleasure of cutting the cord. From that moment forward, my nephew and I have shared a special bond.

A few years later, my sister was diagnosed in the fourth stage of colon cancer. My parents and I took turns being with her while she was receiving chemotherapy treatments which left her feeling tired and sick most of the time. My mother and I had agreed that we were going to wear a wig in the same style as the wig my sister was going to be wearing, but as we planned our show of support, I noticed that my sister's hair had not yet begun to fall out. We later discovered the reason my sister's hair was not shedding was because the chemotherapy treatments were not working.

My sister fought to survive so that she could take care of her nine-year-old son, and my parents and I did all we could to help. My mom was the star player of the family and did so much for us. She made sure we were all taken care of and prepared hot meals for us every day. Until her own health began to fail, my mom was an integral part in helping us all keep it together. With my sister fighting the battle of her life against cancer, and my mother's health also beginning to fail, my world was quickly shifting.

We all gathered at my mom's sister's house for dinner on Christmas day. My mom was in a lot of pain, but she didn't want my aunt to be worried about her. My aunt was quite feeble herself and was barely holding on, so my mom wanted her to focus on her own healing and recovery. She had been very quiet about her sickness, which I believe created an extraordinary amount of stress on my mom. When she announced at dinner that she was in too much pain to fix my dad a plate of food, we all knew that things were drastically getting worse.

In February 2013, I was driving on my way to work and was involved in a car accident. I was rushed to the hospital with severe injuries, and, for a while, I was unable to return to work. A week after my accident, my mother was on her usual trip to the grocery store when she stepped out of the store and fell to the ground. When I received that phone call from my dad, all I could hear was the sadness in his voice.

I remember hearing my mom tell my sister to do all she could to get better because her son needed her. After mom's fall, the family gathered at the hospital to visit her. Her siblings, who were in town at the time, were standing around her bed and after mom said her goodbyes to them, she forced my dad to leave also. My parents had been married for forty-nine years and we were planning a fifty-year anniversary celebration. My dad knew my mom so well, and when she sent him on his way, he had a suspicious feeling about the way she urged him to leave. My mom just wanted to go home peacefully. On February 20, 2013, she passed away, alone in that hospital room, and since that day, nothing has been the same.

The moment I received that call from my dad, it seemed as if I had lost everything. I began to reminisce about how kindhearted my mother had always been, and I thought a lot about some of the things she loved to do. She loved going to the local casinos, and she won big a lot! My sister and I often held onto her winning tickets so she could go home with some money. She used to talk about taking a stretch limousine from D.C. to Atlantic City, but we never had the opportunity to take that trip. Now, whenever my dad wants to go somewhere, I make sure to make the arrangements. I learned to stop putting off what can be done today until tomorrow, because tomorrow is not promised to anyone.

After my mom passed, my sister's condition got worse. We tried holistic medicine, but with no success. Eventually, she had to resign from her job and moved in with my dad. I knew she decided to move in with him because she did not want to be alone, and when she could no longer care for herself, my dad and I became her caregivers. Most days, her pain was unbearable, and it was very difficult to watch my sister suffering. After months of caring for my sister and my nephew, and comforting my dad, I needed to take a break from caring for everyone else. So, when September rolled around, I decided to take trip to New Orleans to celebrate my birthday and get refreshed for the rest of the journey ahead of me. Upon returning from that trip, my sister had to be rushed to the hospital on two occasions. The second time, it seemed to me that she knew she wasn't coming back home. The pain medication that the hospital administered had no effect on her pain and I was emotionally crushed when I heard her tell the doctor "There is nothing you can do for me." I immediately called my dad.

My dad rushed to the hospital with my nephew and as soon as they arrived, my sister was headed to the intensive care unit. After they were done hooking her up to about ten different machines, my sister instructed me to grab a certain piece of paper out of her bag. On that paper were instructions for her funeral service. She had written specific instructions that detailed what she wanted to wear (a white suit), how she wanted her hair to look, what suit my nephew was to wear, and she left instructions for me to see that he got a haircut. On October 13, 2013, my sister passed away. I cherished the letter she had written with her final wishes listed, and I followed it to a tee. Her death came only eight months after my mother's death and because their deaths occurred so close together, the funeral home gave us a discount.

In her forty-two years of life, I was incredibly proud of everything my sister had accomplished. She had a debilitating condition called tri-palsy which left her paralyzed at birth from the neck down. Although she had limited use of one arm, she never allowed that to keep her from doing anything she set her mind to do. She was an excellent driver and loved coming to pick me up in her truck. She had always been a whiz at math, and even though I was the older sister, she helped me with my math homework. She received a master's degree from Strayer University and was able to not only fulfill her dream of becoming an accountant, but she was also able to provide for her son. My sister had a genuine passion for life, and I really do miss our daily chats.

I see my mom and sister as my angels watching over me and my family. We were all very close and I still sense their spirits whenever I find a quiet corner to have a prayerful conversation with them. It is a wonderful experience, so when I'm worried or need advice, I get quiet and listen for their voices. I also get a great deal of comfort when I listen to the soft-spoken words of the voice messages left by them. Some would most likely say I'm crazy or that doesn't make any sense, but my peace is attached to what I believe. To me, it's an amazing experience to be able to communicate with them.

My mom had all her affairs in order when she passed. Her bills were all current and her car was paid in full. When my sister passed, I was named as executor of her estate and the first thing I had to do was hire an estate lawyer to help me navigate the challenges of evicting tenants for non-payment. That process was stressful and filled with time-consuming court dates.

I was still recovering from my near-fatal automobile accident, dealing with the stress of my mother's passing, and concerned for my sister's failing health. Everything associated with losing a loved one was taking an enormous toll on me. I thanked God every day for bringing me through, and with everything that was going on, I sought counseling. My blood sugar numbers were all over the place. I met on a regular basis with counselors who helped me work through some of the common issues associated with grief, such as depression, loss of appetite and sleeplessness, to name a few.

I had to fight to gain lawful possession of my sister's Lexus, and even though the judge ordered the defendant to turn the vehicle over to me that day, it never happened. I determined, after a long fight over its possession, that it was just not worth the stress, aggravation, or the frustration involved. I was able, however, to take over the payments of her truck at a reduced interest rate and when I went to pick up the tags from the DMV, I noticed that the tag numbers were the date of my sister's death. The woman who handed me the tags confirmed what I thought when she said, "These are meant for you."

My sister is resting at Fort Lincoln Cemetery in a mausoleum where I visit her on a regular basis. When the family gathers there on birthdays, the anniversary of their death, or on holidays, I always leave two empty chairs out for them. I still honor my mom and sister.

We hurt badly when we lose our loved ones and there are so many moments that we miss after they are gone, but in the end, what gets me going and through every day is knowing that my mom and sister are in a better place and are no longer suffering.

> "Have I not commanded you? Be strong and courageous. Do not be afraid; do not be discouraged, for the Lord your God will be with you wherever you go."
> -Joshua 1:9 (NIV)

GRIEF BEYOND THE GRAVE
Marsha Witherspoon

On August 5, 2009, I dropped my mom off at her appointment to have some routine bloodwork drawn. In February of that same year, she was diagnosed with acute lymphoblastic leukemia and was admitted into the hospital for twenty-six days of treatment. The treatment worked and she returned to work, cancer free.

As children, we never imagined living life without our moms. As teenagers, we wanted to move out as soon as possible, thinking we were grown and had all the answers. But as adults, the thought of not having our moms here with us is traumatizing, to say the least.

My mom was my friend, my biggest supporter, and at times my worse critic. I grew up in the inner city with three siblings, so being raised by a single parent made it even more difficult to try to navigate through life. My mom and I shared a special bond and as I grew older, she cut the cord and allowed me to find my own path in life. I was her first child to graduate high school and attend college, and when I was a member of Virginia State's Trojan Explosion Marching Band, my mom attended the games to support me.

After I dropped her off for her follow-up doctor's appointment, I went back home to wait for her call to come pick her up. I had just purchased a home that February, when she got her diagnosis, and I was just getting around to having some work done at the house. About an hour or so later, I heard my mom's special ringtone, so I picked up the phone and said "You ready girl?" All I heard on the other end was her crying. My mom had such a tough exterior, so to hear her crying caused me to panic. I quickly pulled the phone away from my ear to look at the screen to make sure it was really my mom on the other end. "What's wrong?" I asked.

"The doctor said I won't be here long, and they need to talk to you."

I felt as if all the air around me was starting to suffocate me. I began to spin around in the middle of the floor while frantically repeating, "I need to get to my Momma!" My uncle, who was there working on the house, was able to calm me down and as soon as I had pulled myself together, I tried to reach my sisters. My oldest sister didn't answer the phone when I called, so I immediately called my other sister. By the time I talked to her, I was crying hysterically as I relayed my mom's message. My sister reacted very calmly, which was what I needed at the time, and after I spoke with her, I called my aunt (my mom's sister) to give her the news. After those phone calls, I left for the hospital.

I had calmed down a bit by the time I got to the hospital and my mom was sitting outside waiting for me. I parked my car and we both went back inside. While waiting for the doctor to step into the examination room, I observed my mom's calm demeanor, but I just had to know what was happening on the inside of her.

"Mom, how do you feel about what the doctor told you?" I asked her.

"Marsha, just take care of my baby," was her only response.

The baby she was referring to was my baby brother who had been incarcerated for the past seven years at that point. Of course, I put her mind at ease by agreeing to take care of him, but in my head, there was another conversation going on.

"Take care of your baby? Um, well what about me? Who is going to take care of me and look out for me!?"

When the doctor finally came into the examination room, he let us both know that the cancer had returned, and my mom had possibly up to three months left to live. I was stunned and confused because according to my mom she didn't feel sick at all! She had returned to work, was working every day, and she certainly didn't look sick! She was given an option by the doctor to either take a chemo pill or do nothing. My mom's decision was to take the chemo pill and go home.

We asked the family to meet at my mom's house so that everyone could hear, in one setting, what the doctor said. My sisters and their children were all gathered with my mom as the news that their mother and grandmother was dying was released. We all were there to process the news in our own way, but my mother gave me specific instructions about what she wanted for her funeral service.

Mom wanted a white casket and she wanted to be buried in the dress she wore to my wedding. Pictures of her two great-grandchildren were to be placed in her casket along with pictures of her two great-grandchildren who were due to be born that upcoming November. My mom continued to have a positive attitude and just wanted to make the next few months memorable ones.

The following day, August 6, was my birthday. Strawberry shortcake was one of my mom's favorites, so instead of celebrating with a traditional birthday cake, we celebrated by eating ice cream and strawberry shortcake together with a few other family members and friends. The next day, my mother and I had scheduled a drive to Maryland to take my daughter there to spend some time with her paternal side of the family. My mother had planned to ride along, but since she had appointments to get additional bloodwork done, I drove from Virginia to Maryland, dropped off my daughter, then drove myself back to Virginia. I was exhausted after that trip, but I wanted to stop by my mom's house to check on her. When I walked into the house, my mom was entertaining a house full of people, had been on the phone for hours talking with her best friend who lived in Texas, and was just chilling like everything was good.

Two days later, on August 8, I received a call from my sister alerting me that my mom was being transported to the hospital by ambulance because the area where her port was located would not stop bleeding. I beat the ambulance to the hospital, so I sat there and waited for it to arrive. When it arrived, I saw my mom and she waved to me.

"I'll catch up with you after you get registered," I told her, as they rolled her into the emergency room. After several hours of waiting, I finally approached one of the triage nurses and asked for an update on my mother.

"What does it mean when the nurse tells you the chaplain will be out to speak to you?" I texted my friend CC. My friend simply replied, "I'm on the way."

I was content to sit back down and wait. Soon after that, my husband at that time and some of my friends began to arrive and after more than an hour of waiting, my name was called. I listened as they were explaining to me my mom's condition, but I was confused.

"Your mom came in and had some problems breathing so we had to put her on the ventilator" they explained to me.

"Wait! I said. "You have to have the wrong patient, let me see your chart. I just saw my mom, she waved at me, and I waved at her. How is she now on a ventilator? She doesn't want to be on a ventilator!"

"Well, I suggest you call your family and friends; give us a few minutes to clean her up and we will call you."

I immediately instructed my friend Chandra to call my mother's best friend in Texas. I told my then husband, to call my aunts and my sisters. It still hadn't registered to me exactly what was happening, so I went outside and sat on the stoop to process what was going on. When I saw my Aunt Frances get out of a car crying, it finally hit me. My mother was a few floors up, dying.

When they finally called us upstairs, my mom was laying there so peacefully. I put Vaseline on her lips, kissed her forehead, and told her I loved her. My Aunt Frances was so overwhelmed when she walked into the room, she almost fainted. My uncles had a similar reaction at the shock of seeing their sister lying there dying. I was still in a place of peace as we stood in a semi-circle around her bed watching her. The nurse came in at some point to check her vitals and announced to everyone there, "I'm sorry, but she is gone."

"How dare she leave me before I could take her off the ventilator!" I thought.

As pandemonium filled that fourth-floor hospital room, I kissed my mom, told her I loved her, and asked the nurse to call the funeral home. My queen, my supporter, my mother was gone. I went home because I needed and wanted to be alone.

Following the death of my mother I busied myself planning a beautiful celebration of life for the one who meant more to me than anyone in this world. I managed every aspect of that celebration. I made all the arrangements, planned the reception, made sure the nieces, nephews, my two older sisters, and my daughter had everything they needed to wear to the funeral, and anything else that needed to be taken care of, I took care of it. When you are busy being busy, who has time to grieve? In two days, I had her whole funeral planned and thanked God for life insurance. On that following Wednesday, I was ready to travel back to Maryland to pick up my nine-year-old and drive her back to Virginia. I was cutting her visit short, and I had the tough task of letting her know that her grandmother had passed away. I was still trying to process things, but I kept busy on my mission to make sure everything was right.

So now what? The funeral is over, the phone calls have stopped, life has return to normal for everyone else, but how do *you* move forward? How do you grieve beyond the grave? How do you begin to live life without that special person? What will become of you? How does grieving look? How does life go on, and what do you do with the time you would normally be talking to the one we loved so much?

I buried my mother on August 15th and two days later I was in class starting my second semester of graduate school. I did not allow myself time to properly grieve and literally took on the role of matriarch for my entire immediate family. For years, I carried the weight of my family on my shoulders because I was always trying to be the strong one. I didn't realize how heavy it was until now.

...TO BE CONTINUED.

> "Everything I am you helped me to be."
> -Unknown

MY MOM, MY FRIEND, MY CHILD
Wilma A. Pinnock

My Mom:

My mom was known as a very sweet and caring Afro-Latina, but make no mistake, she was definitely not a pushover. Even though she only had a fourth-grade education, she was a strong, independent woman who taught me the best lessons on gratitude, respect, and how to appreciate and understand the sacrifices of love. When I was five years old and my sister four, my dad left us in Central America to migrate to the U.S. I don't remember much of my life before the day he left, but my world shifted whether I was aware of it or not. On that warm and sunny day, which is forever embedded in my memory, Mom reassured me and my sister that my dad would come back to get us and bring us to the U.S. to be with him. Mom taught me, by example, to never speak ill about my dad and whenever he sent things to us from the U.S., she insisted we write him a letter expressing our gratitude.

After my dad left for the U.S., seeking the American dream, Mom did everything within her power to shield my sister and I from the elements and environments of our very poor neighborhood. Her street smarts were unmatched, and everyone knew to not even attempt to short-change her. She was known for her no-nonsense attitude, but she had a heart of gold. Taking care of her family was paramount in her life and she never deviated from loving us and taking care of us.

We lived in a 25' x 25' room in a roach infested board building with communal toilets, bathrooms, and sinks. The three of us shared a double-sized bed, and while we may not have had much money, we had each other and we were extremely happy. Our neighbors were the twenty families who lived on the top floor, and the twenty families who lived on the floor below us. Mom was very protective of me and my sister and never let us out of her sight; and she only allowed us to play with the kids who lived in our building.

Working as a maid and babysitter for white American soldiers and their families during the day, it was her sacrifice of love for us which got her up at 6:00 a.m. to walk forty-five minutes to a job that barely paid enough to put food on our table. She practically raised some of the soldier's children, and at the end of the day, Mom would take a bus into the city to pick up my sister and I from either our Tia's (aunt's) or our abuela's (grandmother's) house.

On my tenth birthday, life got much better for our family when mom hit the lottery. She was able to use some of her lottery winnings to rent the vacant room located next to hers. After we painted the walls of that room and put down new linoleum on the floor, my abuela came to live with us. She didn't know I was going to be her roommate, but I was happy to finally have my own bed to sleep in. It was a huge deal to have my abuela move so close to us. She was there to watch over us when Mom left for work in those early hours of the morning, which was another example of how Mom sacrificed to make sure we were well cared for. As I got older, I learned to appreciate the effort and love my mom always exhibited in doing what she did to provide for us. I never heard her complain either– NOT ONCE!

Around my twelfth birthday, a community pool was built in front of our building. I was looking forward to learning to swim, but it took an incredible amount of convincing and assurances from our neighbors that my sister and I were going to be well protected while at the pool. Mom never rested when it came to protecting her girls and she never let us out of her sight! Eventually, Mom saved enough money to move us out of the roach infested rooms we were living in, and while we were glad to be moving, we were saddened to leave behind most of our wonderful neighbors who watched us grow up.

Much to our surprise, a few of the neighbors from our old neighborhood were also able to move into our new complex, which added to the joy. The multi-family, high-rise apartment building we moved into was nice and clean and even had a working elevator. When we moved, we no longer had to share the amenities with everyone in the building--we had our own kitchen, our own sink, and our own toilet. Our new apartment was located on the eighth floor. Mom became a master engineer once we moved in; she divided the one space apartment into three living areas which included a living room, kitchen, and bedroom. What an accomplishment!

At an early age, I really began to realize and appreciate the daily sacrifices Mom consistently made for us. She was a self-taught seamstress at a professional level. Mom could not afford the store patterns, so she learned to draw and cut-out her own dress patterns using newspaper. She bought a Singer sewing machine and did sewing as a side job. Not only did mom design our 15-años dresses, but her one-of-a-kind designer outfits would also have made excellent boutique pieces. Whether casual, our Sunday best, or evening wear, mom made sure her girls always looked their best. For each of our weddings, she designed and sewed our bridesmaid dresses and both of our wedding gowns.

Love is more than just a word. Mom referred to my sister and I as her life. She proved it when she sacrificed her social life to work tirelessly to give each of us her selfless love. My heart overflows when I think of the richness of her love and her eyes which only illuminated for me and my sister.

My Friend:

"I am the adult and you the child; always remember that." That was my mom's constant reminder to us as we were growing up. She never allowed either of us to work, and when we were in school, her mantra was, "School is your only job, and the only job you should have." She was very strict, and I can certainly understand why she had to be that way with us. I never disrespected Mom and I never talked back to her (not that she could hear). I tried to never contradict her...yes, I was afraid of the woman.

With Mom's blessing, I got married at the age of twenty and reluctantly left her in Central America when I migrated to the United States with my husband. When I became pregnant with my first child a couple of years later, I did not know what to expect since

I had never babysat before. Needless to say, I needed help. When I asked Mom to come and assist me, she dropped everything and came to my aid. She hated leaving my abuela alone, but she knew she was the only one who could tend to her first grandchild the right way. Even though I often told her, she really did not comprehend how much I always appreciated her selfless love and care for me and the children. After she made that first trip to the U.S. to assist me, Mom continued to travel back and forth from Central American, up until the time we lost our abuela. Once abuela passed, my sister and I traveled back to Central America for the funeral, packed up our mom, and brought her home with us. There were no ifs, ands, or buts about that!

Our family dynamic changed when Mom migrated to the U.S to live with us. Our family grew to include mom, my three daughters, my husband, and me. We took most of our vacations together, and we helped my mom become acclimated to her new environment. We arraigned for her to continue doing some of the things she loved to do back home like playing bingo. We even convinced her to begin visiting some old friends, taking bus trips or solo vacations with them; all the things she never wanted to do when she was back home. I enjoyed our open conversations, and as an added bonus, my sister and I had a built-in babysitter!

Mom became comfortable in her new environment, venturing out without a chaperone to catch a bus or take a walk wherever she wanted to go. Whenever my sister needed a babysitter, Mom walked to her house, with no questions asked. As the matriarch of our family, the queen of our tribe, the Big Kahuna, Mom continued to thrive as the backbone of our family. My familiarity with the term "it takes a village," became more apparent once my mom moved in with me. Mom did what she was used to doing—she took care of the village.

Mom was the most kind-hearted person. She overextended herself to help others and she never said no when she was asked to do something. Babysitting for our friends was just another way for her to spread her love. Mom chastised the children for misbehaving, cleaned them up, and returned them to their parents potty-trained, clean, and happy. She was very independent, headstrong, beautiful, and full of energy, and as kind as she was, everyone knew not to underestimate her because she would come out swinging! Yes, only a fourth-grade education, but smart! Even though she could not spell the word, mom was an entrepreneur and a fashion icon. Mom was everything, and we knew it!

My Child:

When Mom was eighty, the doctors discovered she had been having repeated mini-strokes, unbeknownst to us or to Mom. That same year, her youngest grandchild, my daughter, was having an away wedding and the family began to wonder how to inform Mom she could not travel or get on a plane to attend the wedding because of the condition of her health. We had already purchased the airline tickets, but Mom's doctors had not cleared her for travel. While we were contemplating about what we should do, Mom informed us of her decision; mainly that she was going to the wedding, and no one was going to stop her. Needless to say, she went to the wedding and had fun.

Wilma A. Pinnock

When we returned home from the wedding, things began to change rather drastically. I noticed Mom was becoming more dependent upon me and she was becoming a lot more fragile. She was still the boss, still the queen and very much respected, but she began moving a lot slower. Four years after her first stroke, Mom needed a lot more care than usual. She was still able to speak coherently and firmly, but she needed the use of a walking cane to get around. Still demanding respect, she continued to enjoy playing bingo, going to parties and talking with her friends on the phone, taking walks with me, and babysitting her grandkids.

When Mom was eighty-five, she had another stroke. That's when I lost my mom and gained a daughter. Becoming less certain of herself and more dependent on me, Mami became my child. Losing a parent to an unexpected condition was difficult and it felt like losing a child in a big mall full of strangers. I didn't know where to begin looking, and the whole time I was searching, I felt lost myself. My mother, who had always given so much to care for the needs of others, needed the village to care for her, and our entire family stepped into the role of caregiver to her. Her daughters, her sons-in-law, her five grandchildren and lots of family and friends became her village.

Mom's physical appearance did not change; she was still beautiful, but she could no longer remember recent conversations. She became increasingly anxious, did not want to stay indoors, but she didn't want to go outside either. She cried unexpantantly and her displays of emotion were extremely unpredictable; she could be happy at 7:00 a.m. and by 10:00 a.m., she was sad. One of her nightly routines were to strip down her bed of the sheets, pillowcases (and sometimes even the mattress), before taking all the drawers out of her dressers, unfolding and then refolding her clothes. What was happening to the lovely, strong, independent, sweet, and energetic person I once knew? Why could I no longer understand the words coming out of her mouth half the time and why was she belching out such obscenities without provocation?

"Mother...mother...MOTHER! Please come, I need your help!" Mami screamed.

The first-time she called me mother, I thought she was kidding with me and wanted some attention, but when I realized it was not a prank, I cried.

"Why are you doing this to me? Why are you taking my mom away? Please bring her back, I do not want this!" I cried out to God.

When Mami's doctor said she was exhibiting all the signs of dementia, I had to look up the word. Although I may have known the meaning in my head, I wanted to verify what I thought I knew. Once I had an understanding of the word, I had to own it, and from that point, there was no turning back.

The National Institute on Aging defines dementia as "the loss of cognitive functioning — thinking, remembering, and reasoning to such an extent that it interferes with a person's daily life and activities." They also say that some people with dementia cannot control their emotions, and their personalities may change. Dementia ranges in severity from the mildest stage, when it is just beginning to affect a person's functioning, to the most severe stage, when the person must depend completely on others for basic activities of living.

Mom was an obsessive bingo player. She would play twenty-seven cards at one time and could still help someone else play their cards. Bingo had always been her game of passion, but the day she forgot how to play bingo, I realized the mother I once knew, was lost. After living with me for over thirty years, she kept saying she wanted to go home. She forgot where she lived, her surroundings, and even her grandkids. She began calling me mother, but she never forgot who I was--I did not allow her to! When Mom began behaving like a two-year old child, I had to begin acting like her parent.

On several occasions I had to send Mom to her room because she was misbehaving. I had to lay out her clothes and have behavioral conversations with her before leaving the house. Yes, I was her mother. For as long as I can remember, I always wanted to be her friend, but being her mother was not a job I asked for, nor was it a job I wanted. Mom had a substantial amount of crystal ornaments she bought or won at bingo. She began hiding them under her bed, in her drawers, or basically anywhere she thought I would not find them. As much as she loved having her hair washed and curled, she would forget we did it that morning and would rewash it that same night. The challenges of caring for her as a child were often disheartening as I watched her slowly fade away. I eventually had to remove the phone from her room and take away her cell phone because she began making calls to family and friends at 2:00 in the morning. Dementia took over her universe and she became increasingly irritated, scared, angry, defiant, and more combative.

There were so many questions we could not answer, and it was very frustrating to know I could not protect my mom from what was to come. The best thing for me to do was to become educated on dementia, Alzheimer's and Parkinson's diseases—basically, anything related to Mom's condition. I researched the diseases and also attended a couple of support groups for enlightenment. I reached out to find support for me and my family as we prepared ourselves to face the unknown. I knew we were not the only family dealing with the effects of dementia within a family, and there was no way I was going down without a fight.

In March of 2021, I was inspired to start my own support group catering to caretakers of loved ones suffering from dementia, Alzheimer's and/or Parkinson's disease. I was aware of some of the challenges which I faced in my own experience while caring for my Mom during the COVID-19 pandemic. I created a one-page information sheet which was handed to First Responders who would in turn hand it over to hospital staff once Mom arrived with no knowledge of where she was. During the pandemic, family members were not allowed to ride in the back of the ambulance, so it was important for us to ensure the paramedics had access to the proper information.

I also formed a support group, "Lean on Me," and brought in several speakers to impart their knowledge about the diseases. Other speakers were also invited to come share their experiences with us, assuring the members of my new support group that they were not alone on their journey. We met on a weekly basis and exchanged stories about our loved ones' latest shenanigans. Occasionally, Mom would swing by and make faces at those participating on the call, but that was just fine. We came to rely on each other for inspiration, comfort, and knowledge. Being a part of the group allowed each of us a space to reenergize for the upcoming week. Best group ever!

Mom started having abdominal pain in June of that same year and was rushed to the hospital. Her dementia became much worse and when we tried bringing her home, she became physically combative and then despondent. Sadly, on September 12, 2021, dementia won, and everything went dark. We lost Mom.

The emptiness and sadness of those last days became incredibly real, and that reality was dreadful. We lost the matriarch and foundation of our family. Learning to deal with the loss of my mom has been a process, and I am still working on being more in tune with accepting the loss. My family now calls me the matriarch, but I have a lot more to learn before I can walk in Mom's shoes. My Mom prepared me for life, and she will always be my mentor and life coach. For as long as I have breath, I will always strive to be half the woman my mother was.

I was inspired by Mom to start my support group. Because of that group, I am stronger and more in tune with the reality of dementia. We continue to meet on a weekly basis to talk about our loved ones and even though my mom is no longer with me, I can still support my group who has now become part of my extended family.

Although Mom is not physically here with me, she still makes her presence known. She will always live on in my heart, and with

Their Blood Runs Thru Us

every tear I shed, I will always remember the day she thanked me for loving her.

I love you, Mom.

"Be the things you loved most about the people who are gone."
-Unknown

EMPATHY, SERVICE AND LOVE

AM Holliday

I stood with my mother and my brother as we patiently waited outside. It was very warm to be a September day in Washington, D.C., and I remember sweating out my recently pressed hair while we stood in line waiting to go inside. I was eleven years old at the time, and when we finally stepped into the building, the air conditioning hit me like a cool wave and I was so happy to be inside. I almost forgot why we were there in the first place...until I saw her.

We entered a large room filled with burgundy velvet-covered chairs in neat rows of six. Walking down the center aisle of that room inside Rhines's Funeral Home, I became a bit confused.

"We must be in the wrong room because that's not my grandma," I thought. She was the first dead person I had ever seen. As we continued to walk down the aisle, moving closer to the pink casket lined with white silk fabric, I said to my mother "That's not my grandma! Who is that?" My mother didn't respond to me. My brother and I stood at the casket with her, holding her hands, and I noticed she had become stiff--frozen. She couldn't acknowledge me or anyone else, so we all stood there and stared at the woman in the white suit lying in the casket, whoever she was. Unlike the petite, light brown-skinned grandmother I knew, her skin was an odd ashen grey color and her face was puffy. A gentle smile on her lips and closed eyes made her look like she was resting. I didn't understand my mother's distress or why we were standing there.

"That's not grandma, is it?" I asked my brother, but before he could answer, Mr. Jones, a family friend, grabbed my brother and me by the shoulders and turned us toward the chairs.

"Sit down," he said.

We waited for the service to start, and we listened to all the good things people had to say about my grandma. Many of them talked about what a good cook she was, how she loved her family, and how much they would miss her. They talked about the nice clothes she liked to wear and how she loved to have parties, dance, and have a good time, but throughout the entire service, my mother didn't move. It didn't dawn on me at the time that she was distraught, I just knew she wouldn't answer us when we tried to talk to her. Finally, my great grandmother caught my eye and gave me the "don't make me come over there look."

"Be still, be quiet, and leave your mother alone or else!" she whispered.

That's exactly what I did.

People loved Dorothea, or Dot as they called her. The love and respect was evident by the many kind words spoken about my grandma, even from those she worked for as a housekeeper. Everyone had only great things to say about her. We loved her too! She spoiled us rotten with candy, homemade cakes and pies and she took us everywhere in DC. I will always remember her taking us to the museums and monuments, including the Museum of American History, the Air and Space Museum and the National Zoo. That's what I wanted to say, but I wasn't allowed, so I sat there and listened as my grandfather talked lovingly about the little woman who migrated from West Virginia to Washington D.C. in the late 1950s to seek more opportunity. He teared up when he talked about how much she would be missed, and how he wished he had more time to spend with her. "Me too Grandpa Jack. Me too."

After the funeral, we went home, and my mother just sat in her room. For two days she didn't do anything, still frozen. One of her cousins came over and stayed with us to help her recover and make sure we went to school and stayed out of trouble. It took over a month before my mother was able to function, but after that, she was never the same again. I was too young to understand the extent of her pain and suffering, but when it became my turn to bury her, I finally understood.

Born on Mother's Day in 1941, my mother, Rose, was a petite woman with beautiful light caramel-colored skin and dark brown eyes. As a child, she was diagnosed with Sydenham chorea, a neurological disease which resulted from a bout of rheumatic fever. Because of the effect that disease had on her body, she required more care than my grandmother was able to provide. Rose's older cousins, Mae and Johnny stepped in to help. They had no children of their own but were known in the community as a couple who cared for other children when their parents couldn't or wouldn't. After some time, my grandmother sent her to live with them. They taught her about farming, how to milk cows, gather eggs from the hens, and how to clean the house. Her Cousin Mae was very strict, which is where Rose learned about discipline and structure.

Rose and the other children in Mae and Johnny's care had to be up, dressed, and finished eating breakfast before dawn. They each had chores to do after breakfast which included hauling water from the well for drinking, washing, and scrubbing floors, and bringing in coal for the stove for the purpose of cooking and heating the house. Rose was born left-handed, which is not a big deal today, but Mae saw it as a problem. Every time she tried to use her left hand, she would get slapped on that hand until she learned how to use her right hand. She learned about God and having empathy for others by going to church, singing in the choir, and reading the bible. Her favorite scriptures were Psalm 23 and Matthew 6:9-13.

When Rose turned fifteen, the house they were living in caught on fire and not long afterwards, Mae died of a heart attack. That's when my grandmother moved her from West Virginia to Washington D.C. Rose loved her new city and rode the bus or walked to explore it whenever she had an opportunity. On one of her many walks of discovery through the city, she met and fell in love with a young mechanic named Melvin. Pregnant at the age of sixteen, Melvin wanted to marry her, but her mother would not allow it. She contracted German measles during her pregnancy, which resulted in her son being born with a severe disability. With the help of her mother and her grandmother, who lived nearby, she grew up quickly, caring for her disabled son while working as a housekeeper and a waitress.

Over the next few years, she was blessed to give birth to my other brother and me.

It was in the late 1960s and she was determined to be her own woman and care for us, and she did it with support from her family and without a spouse. In 1972 Rose married Lewis and began working part-time as a switchboard operator at the Western Hotel in downtown Washington D.C. and, for a little while, our family life was good.

By the time my oldest brother was twelve, it became a lot more difficult for my family to take care of him. It broke my mother's heart when she had to make the difficult decision to entrust his care to an institution which specialized in caring for children with special needs. I could see the pain etched on her face and the sadness in her eyes when he began living apart from us and on the days when we visited him (two or three times a month), she wouldn't smile at all. No matter how hard my little brother and I tried to get her to smile, it never worked. I learned later that she had suffered a nervous breakdown which caused her to completely shut down at times, what I called being frozen. Those moments when she withdrew from everyone and everything, her aunts, uncles and cousins always stepped in to take care of us.

"Your Mom is sick and needs rest," they would tell me and my brother.

"You and your brother have made her sick"

"Your Mom is just tired, she'll be back soon," were some of the non-conversations held about her condition. During that time, it was a common mindset that children were to be seen and not heard and only told things on a need-to-know basis. Despite those bouts of illness and the subsequent divorce from her husband, my mother did the best she could taking care of us, and when we became adults, it was our turn to take care of her.

The shift started in small ways. "What are you doing here baby?" she asked when I entered her apartment.

"Mom, I told you yesterday I was coming over to visit," a little perplexed that she didn't remember the conversation. When my mother smiled at you, it felt like you had just received a special gift; so, she would just smile and we would spend the rest of our time together having pleasant conversations, watching television, going shopping, or visiting my oldest brother. As the shift in her personality became more noticeable, the little things began happening more frequently. It took me a while before I could put two and two together, but I began to take a special interest in some of the things which were beginning to happen.

Mom began calling me on the phone at the oddest hours. It may have been around midnight or 2:00 in the morning, and if I did not answer, she would leave a message:

"Hi baby. Just calling to say hello, love Mom."

When she made those calls early in the morning, I was a little short with her, out of frustration.

"Mom, why are you calling me so early?! I have to go to work!"

"I know baby, I just wanted to hear your voice," she would say.

Those early morning calls always ended with an exchange of "I love yous," and I quickly hung up and then tried to go back to sleep. I was so caught up in my own life that I hadn't paid a lot of attention to some of the other little things she was doing, but I was prompted to take a closer look.

On one occasion I went with her to her doctor's appointment. That's when I found out she had canceled her Medicare insurance and replaced it with another kind of insurance from a company I'd never heard of.

"Mom! What did you do?"

"I don't know."

I decided right then and there to take some time off from work and find out what was going on. I resolved the insurance issue and after a series of MRIs, EEGs, EKGs, and any other test you can think of, we learned that my mother had not only experienced several mini strokes, but she was in the early stages of dementia. Once I recovered from the shock of hearing that diagnosis, I cried to my husband.

"What are we going to do now?" I sobbed.

Mom was an only child, so there were no aunts or uncles to help. I was the only girl in my family and my brothers were unable to help. As we considered our options, my husband and I knew we could not manage her care ourselves because we lived in a townhome that was not wheelchair accessible. We thought about selling our place and finding a good fit for the three of us, but that was a time-consuming process and she needed help right away. While we researched our options and looked for assisted living facilities, we hired a woman to come in every day to help her with chores and make sure she was safe when we weren't there. Every week, we went with my mother from facility to facility looking for one that she might like, and she finally said yes to a nice facility located just outside of the city. It worked because they had a front desk that was staffed 24/7, and no one could enter without permission. The staff would check on her every day, she was protected from the outside world, and she had activities, meals, and community outings available to her. We decorated her new place in the way she wanted, and family members came to visit her regularly. For a while, she was very happy there, but within a year we knew it was time to move her to a place which would offer her more care.

"Mom are you okay?" I asked.

"Hi baby," she said as I entered her apartment.

"You didn't answer the phone, are you okay?" I asked again.

"I'm fine."

I stood there and took a good look at her lying, fully dressed in a wet bed and staring at the ceiling. At that moment I knew she wasn't getting any better, so we gave the facility a 60-day notice and began looking for a nursing home for her. She could no longer live independently and the facility where she lived was not equipped for residents who needed dependent care.

My husband and I spent the next few weeks visiting different nursing homes, comparing costs, and figuring out how much more we would have to pay. Mom's income was very meager; a small social security check that barely covered her living expenses, and nursing homes were very expensive. At the time, the average cost of a semi-private room in a nursing home ranged anywhere from $4,000 to $8,000 a month or more, and if they accepted Medicaid as payment, that would only cover most of the basic costs. Anything falling outside of the description of basic needs (i.e., clothing, cable, telephone, laundry, hair care, toiletries, etc.) was the responsibility of the family. After we completed our nursing home research, we shared the information with our family. They were not very receptive to the idea.

"How can you do that to her?"

"I would never put my mother in a nursing home!"

"Why don't you move her in with you?"

As painful as the family's responses to the idea of my mother going to live in a nursing home were, I understood where they were coming from. They just didn't understand when she didn't sleep for days at a time, would tear the house apart, and write on the walls and talk incessantly about things that didn't make sense. So, I suffered in silence. In my family, we had never sent a sick elder to an assisted living facility or to a nursing home. The strong African American women in my family did whatever was necessary to care for their parents, whether that meant quitting their jobs, working with other family members in shifts, or hiring people to come into the home to help. My own mother had even taken care of other friends and family members, oftentimes without any compensation or reciprocation. I remember the times when she let people stay with us, even if they had to sleep on the floor. Whatever we had, we shared, and in return for her kindness, people often stole from her, took her last dollar or morsel of food, and never looked back.

Before she became too ill to live alone, she let a friend stay with her for a while. That same friend ultimately tried to kick my mother out of her own home! We had to intervene to make her friend move out, but even after that, mom continued to extend herself in helping others whenever she could. The women in my family have a very strong faith in God and people, but often when I went to people for support and help, I was disappointed. Well, I too have a lot of faith in God, but with people I've always been a little more guarded.

Having lived through and witnessed the hardships my mother experienced; I was not eager to repeat them. I was not as selfless as Mom had always been. I sometimes helped people when they needed it, but I wouldn't let their needs have a priority over or jeopardize my well-being or livelihood. Unlike most of the women in my family, I opted to forgo the traditional wife and mother role to pursue a career path. I worked hard and put myself through school while working full-time. I worked my way up from an entry-level government job to a senior-level official and I couldn't just walk away from all of that, could I? I was beginning to doubt myself and feel that something was wrong with me for choosing a career path, but my wonderful husband reassured me that there was nothing wrong with me. I was doing what I deemed best for my mother, and he knew I would never do anything to hurt her. His love, constant support, and encouragement eased my pain and helped me to make the best decision possible for my mom. We moved forward from there.

After weeks of searching, we found a small non-profit, faith-based facility that was able to provide her with a private room and excellent care. Every day after work, I spent time showing her family pictures, keeping her up to speed on everything that was happening in the family, and ensuring she was well and comfortable. During my visits with her, I developed a fond appreciation for *Sally Hansen Quick Dry Nail Polish*. When I polished my mom's nails, I usually sang a little song. As soon as I was done painting her nails, she smiled and immediately touched them, grinning like a naughty little girl and holding them up for me to see. I would smile, clean off the damaged nail and paint it again. Sally Hansen turned an hour-long process into a 20-minute process. Thank you! There were quite a few times when I visited her that she didn't recognize me. When I began to sing the song, she remembered me singing when I painted her nails, she would laugh and sing along. The shift in her cognitive ability was even more pronounced. She would smile, laugh, and sing, but she could no longer remember my name.

Mom lived at that nursing home for a year before suffering a massive heart attack. It was hard seeing her lying there in that hospital bed for four days hooked up to countless wires and machines. My husband and I were there with her on the day before my forty-sixth birthday. The doctor had already told me it wouldn't be much longer for her, so we called the family and we all gathered in her room, held hands and said the Lord's prayer. Right after that, she let out a loud and raspy inhale and when she did, it appeared as if she was raised up for just a moment in the bed. It scared me! My mouth dropped open, but I couldn't say anything. My husband squeezed my hand to assure me that everything would be okay. She then exhaled one last time, and she was gone. I kissed her on her forehead, went into the hallway and cried.

The next few days were a blur. My husband, sister-in-law, and cousin went to Fort Lincoln cemetery with me to plan the service and I was thankful for their help in making the arrangements. I was so numb I barely made it through the meeting. My sister-in-law made the programs, another cousin performed the eulogy, my husband arranged for an accompanist, and my step-sister and other family and friends took care of the repast arrangements. I did not have the capacity or the ability to do anything, and I am forever grateful to them all.

At the funeral, people had so many nice things to say about my mom. They admired her beauty and how she cared for her grandmother, aunts and other family members who needed her care. Everyone had such warm memories of my mother, and they shared them so beautifully. I also had many beautiful memories that I wanted to share. I wanted to share with everyone what an amazing woman she was and how she inspired me to be strong and independent. I wanted to talk about the fond memories I had of our walks to the movie theater to see movies like Sparkle, Buck and the Preacher, and A Piece of the Action, and listening to her favorite songs on the radio by Al Green and Minnie Riperton, and others. In my heart, as I sat there during her service, I wanted to let everyone know how I learned empathy and love from her as I watched her care for my older brother, and other family and friends. There was so much I wanted to say that day, but I couldn't. I was frozen, staring at the pretty casket at the woman in the blue dress inside. "That's not my mother, is it?" It was.

In the year following Mom's death, I struggled. I visited her gravesite almost every week and had a conversation with her as if she were still alive. My husband, whose steadfast love supported me with more patience and grace than I could ever imagine, pulled me close one day trying to help me adjust to a harsh reality.

"Baby, you are killing yourself. Your mom is with the Lord, she is fine."

Then, with as much compassion as he had always shown, he did his best to console me.

"You have got to stop going to the cemetery so much."

I agreed with everything he had said. He was right, and in my heart, I knew it, but my response at the time was an eruption of emotion. I lost it!

"What do you mean!" I screamed. "How can you say that to me? I can't believe you, of all people! I thought you would understand!"

I stormed out of the room, crying and upset.

There are times when the ones who are the closest to us bear the brunt of our full expression of frustration. We can't always see the harm we are inflicting upon ourselves or the ones we love when we become defensive or go on the attack. After I had some time to really process what my husband was saying to me, I was ready to consider his advice. He had always been my biggest advocate and it was time for me to listen more intently to his concerns.

Relationships undergo a real strain during difficult seasons, and it is particularly harder when we allow ourselves to become isolated and refuse to listen to those who love us. I slowly became aware that I should find a different way to grieve. I was so thankful for my husband's caring wisdom and was finally ready to accept the truth in what he said. I apologized for my outbursts and began to decrease the visits to her gravesite.

During a Sunday morning church service, I learned about a faith-based support group with a mission to help people deal with loss. As soon as the service was over, I practically ran to the table in the lobby to sign up. GriefShare is a grief recovery support group which incorporates videos and group discussions about each individual's grief journey. I was initially a little hesitant about sharing my pain in a group setting of strangers, but because I knew I had to do something different, I gave it a try. I became more involved with the GriefShare program and realized that family and friends were not the best at effectively counseling me about grief. As much as they love me, they were not equipped with the proper tools to help me deal with the different stages of grief. GriefShare exposed me to stories of how other people were navigating their grief journey. The participants formed a special bond as we spent time praying, talking, and crying together. We all learned better ways to cope with our loss, we celebrated our newfound strength which enabled each of us to navigate life a little better without our loved one.

It's been over ten years since my mother died and while I still feel the pangs of loss from time to time, I can finally think of her and smile. I fondly remember the love and kindness she gave to her family, her love of movies and music, and her endless selfless acts. I can comfort others who have experienced loss and share some of the coping skills I've learned. I am no longer frozen. I am now free to stand strong and continue her legacy of empathy, service, and love.

"It's Hard to Forget Someone Who Gave You So Much to Remember"
-Anonymous

MOTHA
Katherine McCrary

My heart started racing and I began to feel sick to my stomach. A wave of emotions swept over me as I wondered "how many people know the truth?" Feeling like a fool and the butt of everyone's joke, I was hurt, sad, mad, confused, and felt betrayed. When it was time for school to dismiss, I decided I was going to run away. I had no money and no plan, but I just wanted to escape what I had just discovered.

My fifth-grade class was lined up in the hallway waiting to take a hearing and sight test. We each held our own student file in our hands while we waited to be called to take our test, and I just happened to glance down at my folder. Right next to my mother's name was the word 'foster.' Unsure of what that meant, I turned to my classmate and pointed to the word.

"What does this mean?" I remember asking her.

"FOSTER!" she said loudly.

I gave her a blank stare as I tried to process what I was reading as a barrage of thoughts ran through my mind.

"FOSTER? How is that possible? There isn't any way possible she is my foster mother! This must be a lie!"

I was in a confused daze for the rest of that day. My thoughts kept wandering. My mother had been there for me as long as I could remember, but I found myself wondering how many people looked at my mother and thought to themselves "That is not your daughter." I was in an absolute state of confusion, and as I cried, I began thinking the worst.

When my sister, Iris, tried to explain to me how I became a part of their family, she made a special point to say how special I was and how much my mother and family loved me. At that moment, I saw myself as an outsider. They all belonged together; they were ALL family, not me. From that day forward, in the back of my head, I kept wondering about the other family.

"What if I was with another family? What if I was in a group home? What if my mother would've kept me?"

There was always a longing in my heart to experience more of a bond with my mother. When I visited with some of my girlfriends, I couldn't help but notice how they interacted with their mothers. They discussed puberty, boys, and becoming a woman. Whatever information I received on those subjects was what I got from my sister Iris. She was the one who helped me through my first heartbreak, and when I had my son, she was the one who guided me through the process. Iris was twelve years older than me, and I looked up to her.

To everyone else, my mother was Motha, even to my friends, but to me, she was Mommy. Mommy was a no-nonsense mother and a strict disciplinarian. Chores were expected to be done early Saturday mornings and there was no such thing as back talk. She taught us when we were very young how to cook, and on nights before a holiday, all the food was prepped and ready to be cooked at the crack of dawn.

Although I missed having the same kind of bond with my mother that my friends had with their moms, when I became an adult, I realized how blessed I was to be a part of her family. I talked to my mother every day on my two-hour drive home from work and we always had plenty to talk about. My mother had always been there for me, and she saved me from a life of maybes and unknowns.

I don't know where I would be had she not taken me in, but I am forever grateful for her. It was her strong influence which shaped my life, and I will never forget her discipline. Every Sunday, I was in church, whether I wanted to go or not. When I wanted to sleep in like many of my friends, that was just not happening. Sunday school and church were a given. My mother had a love for God, and she also had a love for bowling. Several days a week she bowled on many different leagues, and I went with her to all the league games.

I knew my mother was sick, and I knew she wasn't immortal, but somehow it just seemed like she was always meant to be here. I didn't think she would leave me, and I felt like I lost two mothers because within six weeks of losing my mother, I lost my sister. I was so blessed for the time I had to spend with them, and I regret that I never told my sister how I really felt about her. I thought I had more time.

My sister Iris was always a ray of sunshine with her upbeat and ready to go personality. She was a diva! She was always dressed as if she was going out on the town and even if she were sick, you would never catch her on a bad day. When my sister was having dialysis treatments three days a week, she was still getting her nails done every other week. When she asked me to visit my mother with her to have family pictures taken, as much as we all didn't want to believe it, we all knew it was the last time we would all get together for a picture with her.

One day, I was driving my sister to get her nails done and the conversation turned to us talking about my mother's funeral arrangements. It was very painful to speak about it, but we both knew it was necessary. While I was talking to my sister about my mother's arrangements, it never occurred to me that we should have been discussing her arrangements as well. I have been to many funerals over my lifetime and for some reason I never thought it would be my mother. She was the last of her sisters and brother and I just never imagined it happening to her. My mother and I traveled a lot while I was growing up. We took a trip to Canada when I was 8 and I remember walking through the streets asking her why those ladies were standing in the window? Back then, I didn't know that was the red-light district. I just remember her saying "Oh, we need to leave, we're going the wrong way." Then she grabbed my hand and covered my eyes. When I think back to all the good she instilled in me, I know I am truly blessed to have been in her life. She was a very important part of my life, and she saved me from so much of the unknown.

Thank you Motha.

"I think about you always, I talk about you still, you have never been forgotten, and you never will. I hold you in my heart, and there you will remain, to walk and guide me through this life, until we meet again"
-Unknown

TIME
Angela Rouson

It's been over 20 years since my mother transitioned from this life to eternity, and there is hardly a single day that passes without a thought of her. She was a slightly suffocating, no-nonsense disciplinarian who dispensed just the right amount of love to keep things balanced; she maintained a family hierarchy that clearly kept her on top. My father was always there but it was clear that my mom was running the show. She did it the best she knew how, and she did it well.

My generation drank from the water hose and played outside until the first flicker of the streetlights. Broken rules, talking back and telling lies were unacceptable and was often met with harsh punishment. Homework was a priority and there was no dating before sixteen, no exceptions. Even with all her rules, she was beyond munificent with her love.

When my mother wasn't shuttling me around to dance or piano lessons, academic programs, or a litany of other random activities, she was constantly dragging me with her to church. Not just Sunday service or Sunday school classes; there were the choir rehearsals, bible studies, and B.T.U. (that's the Baptist Training Union for the young folks out there).

My mother had a quiet strength, and while I'm sure she had failures, struggles and disappointments of her own, she never shared that part of herself with me. I have no memories of her ever yelling or raising her voice to my father, my brother or me, and she somehow seemed to know the right answer to every question. Overly generous and kind, she was also a constant defender, at least where I was concerned.

Once, I complained to my mother that my teacher was being unfair when I received a less than acceptable grade in her class. The real culprit was quite possibly too much socializing on my part, but nevertheless, after my mother had a conversation with my teacher, my grade was changed. My mother was a fierce protector. That was her pattern, who she was and what she did. My dependence on her ran deep, and she clearly swooped in to save me more than she should have, blocking some of the hard blows when they were likely very necessary.

One day I overheard her praying and crying out to God on our behalf, asking Him to help her. It was then that I began to see her as a complete person, more than just my mom. Now that I am older and have children of my own, my biggest regret is not asking her more questions. I want to know about her childhood and what her dreams were. What did she fear in life and what was she most proud of? Was her heart ever broken and how deeply had she loved? I loved her, but still long to know who she was, beyond my mother.

The memories of our time together and the pain of her death have faded over the years,

but she remains a constant presence. I often wonder what type of advice she would give me if

she was still here. Would she be proud of what my life has become? I have thoughts about what she would say about my children, or about the career I have established, and I wonder what her thoughts would be about my once struggling marriage that is still growing in love.

Shortly after college, I married and moved from Florida to Maryland. That time was incredibly hard on my mother because change sometimes is. I was beginning my new life somewhere else, and she knew I had high expectations for my future. When things became difficult to navigate and I could not find my way, she patiently offered a listening ear.

Over the years, my mother and I spoke often, but my visits home became more infrequent. She would visit me when she could, but our time together was not what it should have been. I was getting established in my marriage, engaged in a fulfilling career, and was then pregnant with my first child.

Mom constantly talked about coming up to help when the baby was born and all the things we would do together. She was excited, she was dying, and she knew it.

Recently retired, my mom had plans to relax, have some fun, maybe travel, and expand her social circle. She talked constantly about spending time in Maryland with my little family and our soon-to-come baby boy. One year following my mother's retirement, I received a call from my uncle.

"I was just in Miami and saw your mom. You need to go home."

I went home right away. Life is a moment-by-moment gift from the Creator, and we never know what the next moment will bring. My mom was in the hospital, and when I walked into the room her appearance was unfamiliar. She was bald, bedridden, and slightly incoherent. I showed her a sonogram photo of my baby and she smiled but didn't completely understand what it was. I turned to her doctor and asked what we needed to do.

"There is nothing left to do."

"Well, how much time does she have?"

"She doesn't have any more time."

We never have more time, all we really have is right now.

"I'll be back," I said to my mom before rushing home to prepare to return for a much longer stay. I was seven months pregnant, and the next trip home was for her funeral. I never understood why she kept her cancer diagnosis a secret. I finally confronted my dad to ask why he didn't let me know my mother had terminal cancer and her death imminent.

"She didn't want to worry you. She asked me not to tell."

That was from a man who had always been somewhat cold and emotionally distant from my mother throughout their marriage. I never heard my parents laughing together or saw them share a single kiss. His proclamation of solidarity on behalf of my mother was difficult to understand. I told him that he robbed me of something I could never get back – time. He played a huge part in a seemingly unforgivable transgression, and we didn't speak for a long time after that.

Mom was the glue that held our family together and while her death left us fragile and disconnected, she was loved, and her life was full and worthy of celebration. Dad and I, well, we eventually reconciled.

In the fall of 2019, twenty years after my mother passed, my father became ill. Our relationship was complicated, but many father-daughter relationships can be. I loved him, and I am sure he loved me too. Days before his death, one of his nurses spoke with me about death and dying. She said:

"Death is something that is difficult for people to understand. We fear it and we don't want to talk about it, but death is real. It's part of life, but it is not the end," she said. My dad passed away a few years ago, right before Christmas. His legacy is one of redemption and grace under the most challenging circumstances. I miss my parents deeply, but thankfully, the love never dies.

When someone we love dies, it feels like part of us has died along with them. The world around us and all the people in it just keep moving forward, but our lives feel stuck, and the grief can be all consuming. It is remarkable that we can even go on in the world without their love, and quite frankly, it's astounding that we do. But we get up every day, put one foot in front of the other and move through life the best way we can, right?

What happens when the person you depended on, who celebrated and supported you without judgement passes away? What do you do when the one who sees you, really sees you, leaves? You live.

I want to live to honor the life and legacy my mother left behind. Hers is a legacy of service, giving and love, represented by a life of victory over defeat. Her legacy is one of a woman who fought to the very last moment of her life.

Christ has said in the book of John, "I am the resurrection and the life. Those who believe in me, even though they die, will live, and everyone who lives and believes in me will never die."

He promises, "So it will be with the resurrection of the dead. The body that is sown is perishable, it is raised imperishable; it is sown in dishonor, it is raised in glory; it is sown in weakness, it is raised in power; it is sown a natural body, it is raised a spiritual body."

I will see my mother again and all of my questions will be answered.

My mother's death was painful because I needed more time. We must honor those we love by embracing the time we are given to know them more fully today, and every day that follows.

CALL TO ACTION

The writers and I hope you have found something in these pages that is helpful to you. We have listed a few resources which are available to assist those who have experienced and need help coping with a loss. If you need help, or know of others who may need help, please share this information with them.

If you would like to share your story, I am accepting submissions for the next edition of Their Blood Runs Thru Us. Send an email to theirbloodrunsthruus@gmail.com to learn about submission requirements and to submit your story. Become part of a community that rises from grief by helping others.

Finally, you can find my podcast, U Live After Death (https://anchor.fm/amholliday) on Anchor and Spotify. It's a safe place to continue the conversation about loss and share information. If you would like to share your experience or helpful information with others on the podcast, send an email to ulivaftdth12@gmail.com.

RESOURCES

1. National Suicide and Crisis Lifeline- call, text, or chat 988. 988lifeline.org

2. SAMHSA's National Helpline – Free and confidential advice, 24 hours a day, 7 days a week, for treatment and recovery support services, 800-662-4357 (HELP)

3. Centers for Disease Control and Prevention – Grief and Loss Resources - Grief and Loss (cdc.gov)

4. Center for Prolonged Grief, Columbia University School of Social Work - Complicated Grief Overview | Center for Complicated Grief (columbia.edu)

5. GriefShare – Grief Recovery Support Groups - GriefShare - Grief Recovery Support Groups - GriefShare

6. Johns Hopkins Medicine – Grief and Loss support - Grief and Loss | Johns Hopkins Medicine

7. AARP – Grief, Loss and End of Life – Resources & Articles - Dealing With Grief, Loss and End of Life Planning (aarp.org)

8. Healing After Loss, Daily Meditations for Working Through Grief by *Martha Whitmore Heckman*

ABOUT THE AUTHORS

EBONY SHORT

Ebony Short, MBA, BSN, RN-BC was born and raised in Washington, DC where she was educated in the public school system. She has been married to DeMarco Short for 28 years and the proud Mother of two young adults Lenee' and Michael Short. She is a graduate of the University of the District of Columbia (Bachelor of Science in Nursing) and Strayer University (Master of Business Administration). She has practiced as a Registered Nurse for thirty years. Her experience includes leadership and staff level positions and is currently employed at a Medical Center in the Washington, DC area as a Surgical Nurse Case Manager where she coordinates care for patients living throughout the world who travel to her facility for specialized care.

FELICIA SHINGLER

Felicia Shingler retired from 35–plus years' federal government service with over 25 years as a Writer/Editor, performing writing/editorial functions in all manner of official documentation. During her writing career she assisted federal employees in getting promotions, going through desk audits, and transitioning to a different series.

As Blacks In Government's (BIG) National Communications and Public Relations Chair under 2 administrations (2003 and 2006), she has written countless published articles and served as the executive editor for the member's "BIG Reporter" publication. Shingler also served as National Secretary and sat on the Board of Directors (2011-2014) and was named to BIG's Distinguished Service Hall of Fame, the organization's highest honor. She is a life-member of BIG committed to training aspiring writers.

As a single parent she has successfully raised 2 young men in the DMV and is currently an active member of Mt. Ennon Baptist Church in Clinton, MD.

NIKESHIA PINNOCK HOLT

Nikeshia Pinnock Holt is a Maryland native, born and raised in the beautiful and thriving Prince George's County. She is the youngest of three daughters, and a first generation American of Panamanian parents. She has a bachelor's in Psychology from Bowie State University and a Masters in Developmental Psychology from Howard University.

Nikeshia currently teaches psychology at Bowie State and plans to venture into entrepreneurship. Her dream is to develop a non-profit aimed towards helping and encouraging Black girls to be the best versions of themselves mentally, physically, and emotionally. Nikeshia is a published author in research and is currently working on a developmental and coming of age book for adolescent girls of color. Along with her sister, Nikeshia recently finished her first children's book inspired by her toddler daughter and nephew.

Nikeshia enjoys spending quality time with her family, listening to music, or reading Black urban fictional romance novels.

CHERYL LIVINGSTON

Cheryl is the honored daughter of James E. Hunt and the late Mrs. Lovett Hunt. She was born in San Diego, California and was raised in Washington, DC. Cheryl attended the DC Public Schools and graduated from William McKinley Senior High School. She attended Norfolk State University in Norfolk, Virginia. Cheryl has worked at the Library of Congress for thirty-nine years. Cheryl has received many outstanding performances and awards throughout her career. She retired on January 31, 2023. Cheryl proudly owns a small online business where she is an Independent Nail Stylist for a company called Color Street. She has been a Nail Stylist for a little over a year. Cheryl loves helping and mentoring others on how to have healthy nails.

Cheryl is married to her best friend and lifetime partner Kevin Livingston. Together they have three children, four granddaughters and a special nephew.

MARSHA WITHERSPOON

Marsha Lynette Witherspoon is a native of Richmond VA. Raised in a single-family home she was determined to do something different and be different with the hopes of one day opening and owning her own private practice. Marsha is the CEO and founder of My Legacy Counseling & Consulting Services where she serves as a Licensed Professional Therapist, providing Outpatient Therapy to families and individuals specializing in depression, grief and loss, anxiety, and other diagnosis. Marsha is a proud graduate of Virginia State University with a Bachelor of Science in Sociology and Master of Education in Counseling. Marsha is the mother of a 22 year old daughter Maia and 2 year old granddaughter Alohni.

Marsha is a member of Delta Sigma Theta Sorority Incorporated. When she is not busy serving her community Marsha enjoys traveling, going to the movies, hanging out with friends reading, crocheting and spending time with her family especially her granddaughter, and her 14 great nieces and nephews.

WILMA A. PINNOCK

Wilma A. Pinnock is a proud Afro-Latina with a bilingual multicultural background hailing from Panama City, Central America. She enjoys her position of Lead Public Health Advisor in the Federal Government working with the minority population. She holds a Bachelor's Degree in Business Management, and a Master's in Public Administration from Bowie State University. Wilma is known for her crusader spirit. In March 2021 she established and now leads the *Lean On Me Support Group* for families taking care of their loved ones afflicted with Dementia, Alzheimer's, and/or Parkinson diseases. Her dreams are to continue providing a venue where individuals feel comfortable sharing their weekly stories.

She has been married to her high school sweetheart for forty-five years. She is the mother of three beautiful, well accomplished smart women, and have three adorable grandchildren (one from each). She enjoys meeting new people, traveling, and spending time with her family.

AM HOLLIDAY

Alesha M Holliday is a retired civil servant with over 30 years of experience in administrative operations. Her passion for public service extends to her private life where she serves as a volunteer advocate and legal guardian for disabled adults in the Washington Metropolitan area. She has worked with many charitable organizations including: So, Others Might Eat, Manna, IONA, and the Phyllis Wheatly YWCA, Inc. to combat hunger and homelessness in the Washington DC area. AM serves on the boards of several organizations including the PWYWCA, INC, RCM of Washington, and DT Healthcare Solutions, Inc. In her free time, AM loves to read, attend Broadway Shows, travel and spend time with friends and family.

Mrs. Holliday has a bachelor's degree in Business Management from Trinity University in Washington D.C. She is married to her soulmate Lorenzo and has two children and a granddaughter.

KATHERINE MCCRARY

Katherine McCrary lives in Randallstown MD with her heart and soul Derek, her husband of 12 years. They have a 13-year-old daughter together name Gabriella. Kathy has two sons Kiayre and Sanjay, a stepdaughter Morgan and a grandson Reagan. Kathy enjoys reading, traveling, listening to music, and going on cruises. She loves visiting her family in New York when she has time. She enjoys watching crime and mystery shows, as well as spending time with her family and friends.

ANGELA ROUSON

Angela Rouson was born and raised in Miami, Florida. The daughter of Verdell and Booker T., she currently makes her home in the Washington, DC metropolitan area where she has lived for over 25 years. Angela is an alumna of Hampton University, where she obtained a Bachelor of Science Degree in Marketing Management and is currently pursuing a long-held dream of obtaining her master's degree. With a marketing communications career spanning over two decades, Angela presently serves as a Public Information Officer for Prince George's County Government. She is an avid runner, occasional cyclist, aspiring clean eater, persistent dream chaser and proudly imperfect. A woman of faith, Angela is married to Herbert Rouson (whom she met at Hampton), and they are the insanely proud parents of Herbert III and Alexis, students at the University of Maryland-College Park and Syracuse University respectively.